When Not
to Build

Also by Ray Bowman and Eddy Hall

*When Not to Borrow: Unconventional Financial Wisdom
to Set Your Church Free*

Other Books by Eddy Hall

The Lay Ministry Revolution (with Gary Morsch)
Praying with the Anabaptists: The Secret of Bearing Fruit
(with Marlene Kropf)

When Not to Build

An Architect's Unconventional Wisdom for the Growing Church

Expanded Edition

Ray Bowman and Eddy Hall

Foreword by Charles Arn

Baker Books

A Division of Baker Book House Co
Grand Rapids, Michigan 49516

Published by Baker Books
a division of Baker Book House Company
P.O. Box 6287, Grand Rapids, MI 49516-6287

Printed in the United States of America

Library of Congress Cataloging-in-Publication Data

Bowman, Ray.
   When not to build : an architect's unconventional wisdom for the growing church / Ray Bowman and Eddy Hall ; foreword by Charles Arn.—2nd. ed.
      p.   cm.
  ISBN: 0-8010-9106-3 (paper)
  1. Church facilities—Planning. I. Hall, Eddy. II. Title.
BV604.B68   2000
254'.7—dc21   00-037913

Portions of this book originally appeared in *Leadership, The Leadership Guide to Church Supplies, The Clergy Journal,* and *The Preacher's Magazine.*

Unless otherwise indicated, Scripture quotations are taken from the *Holy Bible,* New Living Translation, copyright © 1996. Used by permission of Tyndale House Publishers, Inc., Wheaton, IL 60189. All rights reserved.

Scripture quotations marked NRSV are taken from the New Revised Standard Version of the Bible, copyright 1989 by the Division of Christian Education of the National Council of Churches of Christ in the USA. Used by permission.

For current information about all releases from Baker Book House, visit our Web site:
http://www.bakerbooks.com

To
James N. Posey
who brought us together
and without whom this book
would not have been written

Contents

Foreword

Let me share a puzzle with you. It's a puzzle that stumped me for years. I knew there had to be an answer but each time I tried to solve it, I became more and more frustrated. Only recently did I experience the "aha!" that comes with a solution, and then it was only when someone more enlightened than I showed me the answer.

Here are the instructions. Connect the nine dots below using only four straight lines without lifting your pencil from the paper. Simple, right? Try it.

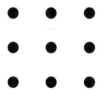

If you have seen the puzzle before and have been shown the "secret solution," it's easy. If you are seeing it for the first time, you probably wonder how, or whether, it can be solved.

Here's a secret that can help you solve the problem. It's the same secret Ray Bowman has used in his wide experience of consulting with churches and the one he brings so insightfully to this book. The secret is: *Don't look for the obvious solution.*

Still stuck? So are a lot of pastors of growing churches when it comes to accommodating the increasing number of people coming to their church. The obvious answer is to build. The wrong answer, for most, is to build.

Can such a paradox be true? Yes. And it won't be the first time.

Jesus, of course, used paradoxes to communicate many insights into the Christian faith:

If your enemy is hungry, give him food.

To be rich, give away your possessions.

To gain your life, lose it.

As I have observed how, when, where, and why churches grow across North America, the paradoxes of growth have also fascinated me:

To attract more people, raise membership requirements.

To grow a group, divide it.

To accommodate your growth in attendance, don't build.

Ray Bowman takes this latter paradox of church growth and explains why it is so. This unusual and perceptive book will bring you the "aha!" experience that will turn night into day, frustration into insight.

The secret: *Don't look for the obvious solution.*

Oh, yes, the puzzle.

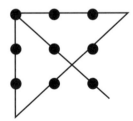

Try it with your friends sometime. Try it on a pastor or lay leader who is considering building a new sanctuary or educational wing. Then give him a copy of this book for the "secret solution."

Charles Arn, President
Church Growth, Inc.
Monrovia, California

Preface to the Second Edition

When Paul Engle, our editor at Baker Books, first suggested we update and expand *When Not to Build,* we weren't sure a new edition was needed. The book was based on principles that we believed were biblical and timeless. Reader responses and continued strong sales made clear that the book's message remained just as relevant as when it had first appeared.

But several changes convinced us that the time for a new edition had come. In the years since the first edition, Eddy Hall and three others have joined Ray Bowman on the church consulting team. Each team member has brought his own experience and perspectives to the consulting work, expanding what the team can offer churches. In the eight years since the first edition was published, all five of us have learned a great deal from our work with churches.

Drawing on these recent experiences, this edition includes four new chapters—5, 9, 10, and 11—plus a new self-test and an additional appendix. We have also updated the original text. For example, this edition uses today's interest rates to compare the cost of building for cash versus that of borrowing to build. We wanted to add enough valuable new information that owners of the first edition would find it worth their while to replace it with this one. At the same time, we didn't want to make the book so big that the price would hinder churches from getting copies for all the board and committee members involved in their strategic planning.

We have witnessed another encouraging change since *When Not to Build* was first published: Churches are more open to its message. Multiple worship services and multiple sessions of Christian education are now standard operating procedure in growing churches. Resistance to converting single-use space to multiple-use space is decreasing. More churches are using these principles, whether they've read the book or not, to get out of debt and stay out of debt, even through a major building program. In all of this, more churches are becoming less focused on buildings and more focused on ministry.

Maybe someday a book like this will no longer be needed, not because the ideas have become outdated, but because concepts considered radical when they were first published have become so universally practiced that no one needs to read a book about them anymore. It will just be the way things are done.

Whether that fantasy will come true, we don't know. But we do know that if your growing church will apply the principles in this book, over time you are likely to save hundreds of thousands or, in some cases, millions of dollars in construction, interest, and building maintenance expense, dollars that will be freed up for ministry. No less important, your staff and lay leaders will avoid the terrible waste of time and energy that would be consumed by unnecessary building programs and they can invest that time and energy in doing the real work of the church.

Every time we work with a congregation and watch them take tangible steps to decrease the time, money, and energy they have to devote to bricks and mortar so they can release these resources for strengthening and expanding the ministries of the church, we find it exciting. May this excitement come to your church next.

Introduction

Fifteen Questions before You Begin

Sunday mornings your worship space is filled to 90 percent capacity. The older teen and young married classes have standing room only. The fellowship hall can no longer seat everyone at once during your potluck dinners. Obviously it's time to build.

Or is it?

For most churches in this situation, the answer is no. Certainly such a church has urgent facility needs, but a major building program is only one of many options for meeting those needs. Rarely is it the best one.

When a church asks me (Ray) to help them assess their building needs, I often ask the pastor and board members to fill out a questionnaire to help identify motivations for building and gauge the congregation's need and readiness for a major building program.

If you think the time may have come for your church to build, answer each of the following questions *yes, no,* or *maybe.*

____ 1. Do you expect a new building to attract new people to the church?

____ 2. Is it your goal to design a building that will inspire people to worship?

___ 3. Do you expect your members to be more motivated to reach out to others once you have a new building?

___ 4. Do you think a building program will motivate your people to give more generously to the work of the church?

___ 5. Do you expect the building program to unify your people behind a significant challenge?

___ 6. Do you hope that a building program will involve more people in the work of the church?

___ 7. Do you see the building as a way to make a statement to the community about the church's importance?

___ 8. Do you hope that a new building will help your people take more pride in their church?

___ 9. Do you need a larger sanctuary so the entire congregation can worship together at one time?

___10. Do you need to add more educational space so all your classes can meet at once?

___11. Is it possible that your space needs could be met through more creative use of your present facilities, such as converting space to multiple use, changing furnishings, scheduling services and ministries at alternate times, or using off-campus meeting space?

___12. Are you still paying off debt on your last building?

___13. Would you have to borrow a major part of the finances for a building program?

___14. Would payment for the project depend on the church's future growth?

___15. To help pay for the building, would you explore ways to cut spending on your present ministry programs or staffing?

Now, add up your answers. Every *yes* or *maybe* is a possible reason not to build, to delay building, or to seek another more appropriate solution through prayer, research, and reevaluation.

Questions 1 through 8 relate to motivations for building. These issues are discussed in part 1 of this book, "The Principle of Focus." Questions 9 through 11 deal with how best to meet space needs, the subject of part 2, "The Principle of Use." Questions 12 through 15 address financial readiness, which is covered in part 3, "The Principle of Provision."

It is probably already obvious how some of these fifteen issues should influence your decision to build soon, wait a while, or pursue alternatives. By the time you finish studying the first fourteen chapters of this book, you should understand clearly why your answer to each of these questions is important to your facility decisions.

The principles of focus, use, and provision can help your church avoid a premature or unnecessary building program, but if your church continues to grow, the time to build probably will come. Part 4 of the book, "When It's Time to Build," explains who should plan your new building (most churches ask the wrong people to do it) and describes innovative design features that can make your facility a more effective ministry tool.

Finally, an appendix turns the whole book into a working handbook for the congregation that is ready to develop a master facility plan.

If you are looking for ways to fine-tune the church's traditional ways of thinking about, using, and paying for church buildings, this book will not answer your questions. It does not offer traditional solutions.

But if you are among the growing number who uneasily wonder if the church spends too much of its time, money, and energy on buildings; if you feel there must be a better way, a way that would free the church to redirect many of its human and financial resources to meeting the needs of people; if you have ever wished someone could show you and your congregation a proven, workable plan for doing that, then read on. This book is for you.

17

1

Confessions of a Surprised Architect

When a suburban Philadelphia congregation asked me to design a thousand-seat sanctuary, that's exactly what I (Ray) intended to do. They had called me for the usual reasons. Their sanctuary was full and they were running out of educational space. It was time to build.

To determine how best to design their facility, I first met with the church board for four hours on a Saturday morning. Next I spent several days studying the church's ministries, finances, and use of facilities. Then I met with the church-growth committee. Finally, I was sure I had the facts I needed to draft my proposal.

I met with the board again the following Saturday. "What you really need to build," I announced, "is a storage shed."

Had the church invited me a year and a half earlier, I would have designed a thousand-seat sanctuary and cheered them on. "The building will bring more people to Christ," I would have said. "Its beauty will draw you closer to God. People will notice you're here and that you're an important part of the community."

During thirty years of designing church buildings, I had heard all these claims from pastors and church boards and saw no reason not to accept their assumption that bigger buildings translated into greater ministry. But then my life took a surprising turn that made me look at the church through new eyes and forced me to rethink the conventional wisdom that had guided three decades of work.

In 1979 if anyone had suggested I would soon change careers, I would probably have laughed. I had studied to be an architect, spent all my working life as an architect, and after building my own firm and spending twenty-six years as a principal had no intention of ever being anything but an architect.

Then one day as I was driving to our Twin Falls, Idaho, office to meet with one of my partners, a thought came to me as clearly as if someone had entered the car and spoken to me: "There's going to be a big change in your life and it's going to involve your profession." I recognized the voice. When I got home, I told my wife, Sally, about it, then promptly forgot it.

Three weeks later I had a totally unexpected opportunity to leave my architectural firm when one of my partners, over lunch, offered to buy my stock. I had absolutely no idea what prompted his offer. When I told Sally about it, she said, "No way!" But as we prayed about it, both Sally and I felt we should accept.

"But, Lord," I said, "then I'll have no work and no income. What am I supposed to do?"

God's answer was clear even if a bit sketchy on details: "I'll show you what kind of work you are to do and give you all the work you can handle." On the strength of that promise I accepted my partner's offer and left behind an established career for an unknown future.

The day after I signed the papers dissolving my association with the firm, Sally and I were on our way to Canada for our first consulting job. A church in Red Deer, Alberta, had asked me to conduct a feasibility study to determine whether they should renovate their existing building or relocate to a larger site. Though it was just my first day to wear my consultant hat, I felt at once the difference it made. Even if the church were to decide to build, I knew I would not be their architect. I don't suppose the possibility of advising a church *not* to build had ever crossed my mind before. But at Red Deer, for the first time, it was a live option.

When I was an architect, my job had been to follow instructions, to design whatever kind of building the church asked for. When I became a consultant, though, my job changed. I had to advise the church on what was best for the church and that meant looking at the big picture. I analyzed the church's finances. I charted growth patterns. I studied utilization patterns of the existing building. At Red Deer I ended up advising the church to remodel and grow right where they were.

But the biggest surprise of that consultation came as I was about to leave. "Ray," the pastor said, "do you know what you are?"

"No," I answered, "I really don't."

"What you are," he said, "is a church-growth specialist."

And though that thought was totally new to me, it rang true. God had called me to invest the next chapter of my life in helping churches reach out more effectively.

That didn't mean, however, that I had the expertise my new role demanded, a point soon driven home when another church board peppered me with church-growth questions I couldn't answer. So for the next year I spent much of my time between consultations reading about ministry and church growth, listening to tapes, and asking the Holy Spirit to teach me. I began to relate what I was learning about church growth to what I already knew about architectural design. I studied church finance and was surprised to learn that the Bible clearly describes financial principles that can guide the work of the church, principles much different from those followed by the world—and most churches.

So by the time the Philadelphia church asked for my help, I realized that a facility plan intended to maximize ministry could not be created in a vacuum. It had to be developed hand in hand with a ministry plan and a financial plan. All three had to work together. Because I had looked at the church's facility needs not in isolation but in light of ministry and finances, I had come to a conclusion that was startling, at least to me: A major building program at that time would in all likelihood stop the church's growth and create financial bondage for years to come.

Over the next ten years I went on to consult with scores of churches and learned from each of them. Because I asked facility questions from a new perspective, from the perspective of ministry and outreach, time after time I was forced to admit that some point of conventional wisdom I had embraced as an architect was untrue. Much of this conventional wisdom encouraged churches to build too big, build too soon, or build the wrong kind of building.

After thirty years of designing and encouraging churches to build new church buildings, it was painful to admit how much of my well-intentioned advice had been misguided. I could see how some churches had actually been hurt by the building programs I had helped with. Some building programs had diverted attention from meeting peoples' needs. Other churches had taken on building debts that financially crippled their ministries. In many cases the building program had slowed or stopped the growth that had prompted the new building.

These hard lessons eventually pushed me to a conclusion so unconventional that it sounds like architectural heresy: Most churches thinking of building shouldn't, at least not yet. I became convinced, in fact, that the single most valuable lesson a church can learn about building is *when not to build.*

And that lesson can be summarized in three parts—three situations in which a church should not build.

When the Reasons for Building Are Wrong

First, a church should not build if its reasons for building are wrong. Richard Foster describes a congregational meeting his church held to pray for God's guidance concerning a proposed building program. "I went into the meeting thinking that probably we should build, and left certain that we should not," Foster writes. "The crucial turning point came when I saw the driving force behind my desiring that building to be my unarticulated feeling that a building program was the sign of a successful pastor. Theologically and philosophically, I did not believe that, but as we worshiped the Lord, the true condition of my heart was revealed. Eventually, we decided against building, a decision now validated by hindsight."[1]

Years ago a church of about 150 people in Arkansas hired me as an architect to design a new sanctuary for them. When I saw their building, I was puzzled. Though the building was older, its location was good and the congregation had never filled it.

Finally, I asked the pastor, "Why do you want a new building?"

"The first reason," he answered, "is that these people haven't done anything significant for twenty-five years. This is a way to get them to do something significant. Second, the people aren't giving at anywhere near the level they could or should be. A building program would motivate them to give more. Third, a building program will unite the people behind a common goal."

I believed he was right on all three counts and designed the new sanctuary. Now I know that this pastor was trying to do something that never works—solve nonbuilding problems with a building. That church built for the wrong reasons.

When There Is a Better, Less Costly Solution

Second, a church should not build when there is a better way to meet space needs. As I studied the Philadelphia church, I agreed at once that it had a space problem. At its rate of growth, the congregation would soon outgrow its worship space. Between Sunday school and their Christian school, their educational space was full. They had no room for additional staff offices. Building was the obvious solution, and I was tempted to lapse into my traditional architect role to produce the design.

But I couldn't. By that time I knew that was the wrong answer. "I found a room filled with missionary boxes," I told the board. "Now, those boxes don't need heat. They don't need windows or carpet, do they?" I recommended a low-cost storage and maintenance building to free up existing space for educational use.

"This barn on your property is a historic structure," I told them. "It's worth preserving. But you're not getting good use out of it." Then we discussed how they could remodel it into a gymnasium, kitchen, and educational space at half the cost of a comparable new structure.

"You can meet your need for worship space for years to come," I went on, "without the tremendous commitment of time, energy, and money involved in building a new sanctuary." The wall between the existing sanctuary and foyer could be removed to enlarge the worship area. A modest addition could provide them with a new, larger foyer, one that would make it practical to hold two Sunday morning services, thereby doubling their worship seating capacity. The new addition could also house the office space they would soon need for their growing staff.

Finally, I suggested they replace the fixed worship seating with movable seating. For the comparatively low cost of new chairs, the church could use the largest single space in the building for a wide range of activities—space that would otherwise lie useless for all but a few hours a week.

The church accepted the suggestions and completed their remodeling and modest construction projects within a couple of years. The church continued to reach out to the unchurched and within six years grew from 300 to 850.

At this church I first began to realize that of the many churches that had hired me to design new buildings, few actually needed them. Most needed to find ways to use their existing buildings more effectively. While fully using space may sometimes require remodeling, refurnishing, or making modest additions, in many cases it requires no money at all, only a willingness to do things differently. What seems obvious to me now came then as a fresh revelation: Until a church is fully using the space it has, it does not need more.

When the Church Risks Financial Bondage

Third, a church should not build when building would increase the risk of financial bondage. A congregation of about 175 in the Seattle area brought me in as a consultant, but only after they had put up the shell of their new building. Someone had offered the church a piece of land visible from the interstate at a bargain price. The church had jumped at it.

Confident that an attractive, highly visible building would make a strong statement to the community about the church's importance and would stimulate growth, they were building a luxurious thousand-seat sanctuary. "We didn't want the inconvenience of building in phases," the pastor explained, "so we decided to build it all at once. I believe that if we just have the faith and the vision, God will provide the money."

25

By the time I arrived on the scene, the church, for all practical purposes, was bankrupt. All I could do was empathize with them and sadly recommend that they board up the unfinished shell, keep on using their old building, and concentrate on growth until future developments enabled them to complete their move.

The Philadelphia church faced a similar risk. When they commissioned my study, they were still in debt for their existing building and planned to borrow most of the money for their new one. This would mean taking on loan payments larger than the congregation could meet, on the assumption that future growth would enable them to repay the loan.

Afraid this could endanger the church's growing edge, I prepared a detailed financial analysis that projected the potential impact of such a decision on the ministry and growth of the church. After extensive discussions the church leaders concluded such indebtedness risked not only the church's future growth but even its existing ministries. The church then adopted a plan to pay off its debt and move toward building future facilities debt free.

Three Principles

These three situations in which it is a mistake to build—when a church's reason for building is wrong, when there is a better way to meet space needs, and when building would risk financial bondage—suggest three positive principles. These principles can guide churches in determining whether it is time to build (the time to build *does* come) and what to do in the meantime, when building is premature.

> 1. *The Principle of Focus.* A church should build only when it can do so without shifting its focus from ministering to people to building a building.

2. *The Principle of Use.* A church needs more space only when it is fully using the space it already has.

3. *The Principle of Provision.* A church should build only when it can do so within the income God has provided and without using funds needed for the church's present and future ministries to people.

These three principles, which the following chapters explain and illustrate, have for two decades guided my work with growing churches. Each year I see more evidence of their power to unleash the church to do its real work. They have enabled congregations to leave behind limiting ways of thinking about, using, and paying for church buildings in favor of ways that free up most of the time, money, and energy traditionally invested in buildings. These resources can then be redirected to the true mission of the church: ministering to the needs of people in Christ's name.

It can happen in your church too.

The Principle
of Focus

*A church should build only when
it can do so without shifting its focus
from ministering to people
to building a building.*

2

Can Buildings Kill Church Growth?

After organizing with 48 members in 1947, Champlain Church[1] grew within four years to 116 members, pushing the limits of its rented facility. To have room for continuous growth, the church took the next logical step. They built. But then a surprising thing happened. Immediately Champlain Church stopped growing. Membership hovered between 90 and 115 until finally, 23 years later, the church's membership loss was restored. As the graph on the next page shows, it was not until 1980, 29 years after the building program, that the growth of the church resumed.

While conventional wisdom says that church buildings create growth, the experience of Champlain Church is actually more common: Church buildings often kill church growth. In over forty years as a church architect and consultant, I have seen it happen time and again. An exciting, growing congregation builds to make room for continued growth, only to see their growth stop as soon as they build.

Growth at the Champlain Church

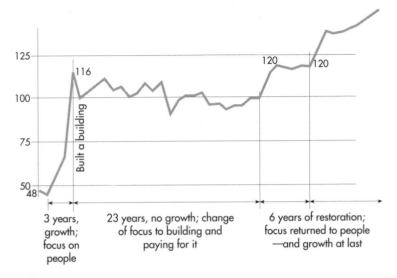

3 years, growth; focus on people

23 years, no growth; change of focus to building and paying for it

6 years of restoration; focus returned to people —and growth at last

A Shift in Focus

Now, I'm not against church buildings. After all, I am an architect. I have designed buildings for churches most of my life. There is a right time and a right way to build. But in far too many cases building programs have killed or at least slowed the growth of vital congregations. Why?

A major reason is that the church's focus changes. Most church growth occurs because a church effectively ministers to people's needs. Its focus is on people. But often, when a growing church builds, its focus shifts from people to building. That change of focus kills church growth.

Take, for example, Grace Community Church, a suburban congregation in a large Midwest metropolitan area. In the seventies their attendance grew from 200 to 1,500. During this period, they built a 1,000-seat worship space that corresponded to their needs and resources but did not interrupt their growth. But before this building was paid for, the congregation decided to build again so they wouldn't have to keep holding double services on Sunday morning. They built a 4,000-seat worship area and have had little growth since.

For years now the people of Grace Community have worshiped in a space more than half empty. In more than a decade, seldom has a Sunday passed when the pastor has not appealed for funds to pay the mortgage. One member who normally would have invited his friends to church told me, "I'd be embarrassed to invite any of my friends to our church, because they'd think the only reason I invited them was to get them to help pay the debt."

Recently I visited with a wonderful retired couple from that congregation. I knew something of the years of devoted service they had given the church, often behind the scenes. "We feel so privileged to have been a part of the ministry of the church," they told me. Then they went on to describe how they had been able to generously support the church's building programs.

Though I didn't tell them, I was saddened by what they said. They had given their lives in loving service to God and others yet they measured their servanthood, not by the many lives they had touched with God's love, but by dollars given to building programs. After years of hearing their pastor appeal for money for buildings, they, and doubtless many others in the congregation, had come to view the building itself as the work of the church. While the church had continued to serve its members, the major focus of the church had become paying for the building. That change of focus had helped kill the church's growth.

At Grace Community the change of focus came about primarily through too much debt, but that's not the only way it can happen. A church of 200 in New York had outgrown both its worship and educational space. They asked me to develop a facility plan that would give them room to keep growing. After studying their situation, I proposed a combination of remodeling and utilization changes that would require little or no indebtedness yet provide the space they needed.

But I cautioned the pastor on one point. "Paul," I said, "I know you have people in this congregation who have the skills to do this remodeling themselves. Because you want to keep putting your funds into the ministries that have been so effective, it will be tempting to let your people do the remodeling. Don't let them. Hire someone to do it for you. Otherwise, the time and energy your people now put into caring for the homeless, for runaways, and for other displaced people will be diverted to the building. It will change your church's focus, and your ministry will suffer."

The church adopted my recommendations on every point but one: The people decided to do the remodeling themselves. Two years later I had lunch with that pastor. "Ray," he said, "you were right. We did the remodeling ourselves, and it changed our focus."

Three years later the church had begun to grow again but it still had not recovered its lost momentum. The change of focus had crippled the church's ministry and interrupted its growth.

A building program can change a church's focus even before construction begins. An established urban congregation of 300 built a multipurpose building used for worship on Sunday and as a gymnasium and for a host of other events during the week. They regarded this gymnasium as a temporary building to be replaced as soon as possible by a "real sanctuary." During the next six years, the church grew to 700. At that point the church's leaders spent three years planning and raising funds for a major building program. During those three years, the church's growth slowed almost to zero. Why?

Unlike Grace Community, the problem was not indebtedness. While the building would stretch the church financially, the leaders were careful not to commit so much to the building that it would endanger the staffing and funding of ministry programs. And unlike the New York congregation, the problem was not that the people did the actual construction themselves. Rather, the church's leaders put so much time and energy into planning the building and raising funds that it changed the church's focus.

The truth is the church already had plenty of room to grow. By adding a third worship service and adding Christian education classes at nontraditional times, the church could have grown to 1,400 or 1,500 in their existing building. Instead, the church decided to build, diverting the leaders' best creative energy to the building program even before the building began.

This changed focus was also evident among the members. When asked how the church was doing, members usually told how the building program was going and often expressed impatience with the process. They honestly believed the church could not move ahead until the new building was finished. The building program, rather than motivating members to reach out, tended to put the church's ministries on hold.

It has been several years since this church completed its new building. Although the new building—the enlarged physical plant—created the illusion of growth, in the years during and following the building program, the congregation has not grown. For yet one more church, building a building became an unfortunate substitute for the church's real work.

Keeping the Focus on Ministry

Planning a building, constructing a building, paying for a building—any of these can become substitutes for ministry, though no church would ever set out to make that happen. Whenever building is allowed to become a church's focus, even temporarily, the church's ministries suffer, and growth slows or stops.

Building, however, does not have to hurt the church. A church can keep its focus on ministry, even through planning, constructing, and paying for a building. The first step in making that happen is for the congregation and its leaders, even before they enter the planning phase of building, to commit themselves to the principle of focus: *Our church will build only when we can do so without changing our focus from ministry to building.*

In 1981 a couple went to a small community on Cape Cod to start a church. While the pastor worked as a plumber to support his family, he and his family began to invite their non-Christian neighbors to a Bible study in their home. Before long they had to add a second Bible study.

Within a couple of years the church grew to about fifty adults who worshiped in the Odd Fellows Lodge building and about thirty children who met in the Masonic Lodge up the street. The church needed more space, and there was no larger space in town they could rent. So they bought land and asked me to help with building plans.

After studying their situation, I was convinced that a building program at that time would stop the church's growth. I recommended that the church set a goal of growing to 150 before building. My experience had taught me that a church needs 50 giving units—150 to 200 people—before it is financially strong enough to build without handicapping its ministry.

Still the church had to have more space right away. To meet that need, I recommended two changes. First, the church should go to double services. Second, the basement of the Odd Fellows building was lying unused, and in its existing form it was unusable. I suggested that the church offer to remodel and redecorate the basement at church expense in exchange for the owners' permission to use the space.

I also suggested three financial goals for the church. First, pay off the remaining $20,000 debt on the parsonage as soon as possible. Second, pay off the mortgage on the building site. Third, accumulate as large a building fund as possible before building.

The church continued to grow, enduring tremendous inconveniences and frustrations because they met in a building barely adequate for their needs. The temptation to build before they were financially ready must have been tremendous. Yet the people persevered, making do with rented facilities until they could build without endangering salaries and ministries.

After five years the church had grown to 150 and had reached all three of the financial goals necessary to enable them to build. They had paid off the parsonage and land and had accumulated a substantial growth fund. By this time they had absolutely no more room to grow. It was time to build.

When the church broke ground in 1988, the pastor knew the building program would not jeopardize the church's ministries.

Yes, building can kill a church's growth but it doesn't have to. A growing church *can* plan and pay for a building program in such a way that the members never take their focus off meeting the needs of people. The way to accomplish this is neither difficult nor mysterious, as the following chapters show. It just calls for a bit of unconventional wisdom.

3

The Myth of Sacred Space

It was an architect's dream come true. First Church had the money to do it right. The building committee gave me the freedom to incorporate into the design everything I believed a sanctuary should be. This was the opportunity I'd been waiting for—the chance to design the ultimate sanctuary.

I didn't have to think twice to know what I wanted to capture in that sanctuary's design. Years of architectural training, many more years of practical experience specializing in church architecture, and my own love for the beauty of the great historic sanctuaries—all these had prepared me for this moment. I was ready.

I told the building committee what I had told dozens of building committees before: "The sanctuary is the heart of the church, a sacred space devoted exclusively to the worship of God. Building your sanctuary should take priority over all the church's building needs. Until you have such a sanctuary, the church's worship will never be all it should be."

The committee enthusiastically supported my proposal, and I set out to design the sanctuary of my dreams. The building I would design would make people want to attend First Church. Once they were there, the environment would speak to their spirits. The stained glass, the pipe organ, the strong vertical lines, the dynamic symmetry—more than mere aesthetics, these design elements would draw people to God, inspire them to worship. And through worship they would be changed. No mere bricks and mortar, this building; no, it would be a means of grace.

My confidence in the power of architecture was hardly unusual. During my architectural training, I had been taught, as most architects are, that the key to solving social problems was to create new and better environments in which to live, work, learn, and, in my case, worship. Though I would not discover it for several years, there was a problem with that belief: It was wrong.

That realization came gradually. A church in Nampa, Idaho, asked me to design a worship space for them with a multi-level platform, movable choir seats, portable risers, and ramps to make it easy to move props and equipment on and off stage. They envisioned using the space for dramas at Christmas and Easter, for a symphony orchestra, for big or small choirs that could be moved to various locations. With the experience of designing that sanctuary, cracks began to appear in my traditional thinking.

Three years later I designed my first totally flexible church facility. Worship, Sunday school, fellowship, and recreation all took place in the same area. The building had no "sacred space"—space set aside exclusively for worship. Though the congregation saw this building as temporary, to be replaced later by a single-use sanctuary, in designing that building I became a bit more open to new possibilities.

My traditional thinking was further challenged when I left my architectural firm to become a consultant. Because I wanted to help churches do facility planning in a biblical context, I spent a lot of time studying the New Testament. What I found startled me.

First, I discovered that *sanctuary* is an Old Testament concept that was abolished in Christ. *Sanctuary* means "where God dwells," and in the Old Testament the Holy of Holies was indeed a special dwelling place for God. But when Jesus breathed his last on the cross, the curtain of the temple tore from top to bottom and opened the Holy of Holies—where God dwelled—to all humanity.

Scripture leaves no doubt about where God dwelled from that moment on:

> [God] doesn't live in man-made temples (Acts 17:24).
>
> Don't you realize that all of you together are the temple of God and that the Spirit of God lives in you? (1 Cor. 3:16).
>
> Your body is the temple of the Holy Spirit (1 Cor. 6:19).
>
> We are his house, built on the foundation of the apostles and the prophets. And the cornerstone is Christ Jesus himself. We who believe are carefully joined together, becoming a holy temple for the Lord (Eph. 2:20–21).
>
> And now God is building you, as living stones, into his spiritual temple (1 Peter 2:5).

All my life I had heard that the church building, especially the sanctuary, was "God's house." Had I lived before Christ's earthly ministry, it might have been appropriate to give that kind of reverence to the temple. But my Bible study now convinced me that my thinking was two thousand years out of date. As Jesus explained to the woman at the well, it's not *where* we worship that counts, but *how* we worship (see John 4:21–24).

For the first time I realized no human could ever design a sanctuary. No amount of money, no amount of stained glass and carpet and padded pews could transform bricks and mortar into the dwelling place of God. God has already chosen his dwelling place and he has chosen not "man-made temples" but the hearts of his people.

Second, my Bible study showed me that the New Testament church owned no church buildings, though they held both large-group and small-group meetings. The large-group gatherings, for the most part, were not meetings of the church—believers—but rather meetings for public evangelism, something like today's evangelistic crusades. Such public evangelism took place in the temple courts, in a public market, in synagogues, in a rented hall, on a riverbank. It seems never to have crossed the apostles' minds that they might need to build large auditoriums to conduct public evangelism. Meeting space already existed, and besides, these evangelistic crusades were not ongoing year-round meetings but rather part of the church-planting process. Once a church was established, the large evangelistic meetings were succeeded by a network of house churches in which the believers worshiped together and ministered to one another.

In Jerusalem people came to Christ by the tens of thousands and possibly hundreds of thousands. In our day such rapid growth would promptly run into obstacles. Where could we find facilities large enough for all those people to meet? Even the temple courts would have been overrun quickly had they all tried to meet together. But meeting space was no problem for those first Christians, because as more people became Christians, more homes—thousands of them—became available as meeting places.

The first-century church prayed, taught, evangelized, healed, baptized, ate together, celebrated the Lord's Supper, shared to meet the needs of others, sang, worshiped, and praised God. And they did it all without owning a single church building.

For almost three centuries the church built few if any buildings, and it continued to enjoy the most vigorous period of ministry and growth the church has ever known. Then disaster struck. Constantine declared Christianity the state religion.

The church became less and less a community of believers, more and more a religious institution. The church built buildings and more buildings. Its focus had shifted. The church's most dynamic era had come to an end.

Now, I know the gospel is supposed to be good news, but for an architect, especially for an architect who had already invested most of a lifetime in designing church buildings, my biblical findings did not much feel like good news. I found it hard to admit my mistakes, to concede that much of my life's work had been misguided. Had my decades of service to the church as an architect been wasted? Even more important, were my training and experience of any further use to the church? Or was the whole idea of a "church architect" inconsistent with a New Testament vision of church, a church without sanctuaries?

In time I found comfort in this thought: The church needs buildings. Whether borrowed, rented, shared, leased, built, or bought, the church will always need buildings. What would happen, I wondered, if I left behind my arrogant belief that I could design a building that would somehow draw people to God, cause them to worship, inspire them to change? What if I started with the idea that the church is people and its mission is to meet the needs of people in Christ's name? What kind of building would result?

To find an answer I looked to the words of Christ. I noticed that he continually described himself and his kingdom with words such as *meek, lowly, kind, merciful, good, just,* and *humble.* What kind of design, I wondered, would reflect these values?

Personally, I loved Gothic architecture with its ornate grandeur, but it clearly did not reflect the values of Jesus. Rather, it was a monument to the pride and power of humanity. A design based on Jesus' values would not be ornate but simple; it would not be pretentious but restrained. The space would not overpower people with its lavishness or size but would make them feel welcome and comfortable. The very style of the architecture would say that people are more important than the building itself.

I also looked around at growing churches for clues. Most growing churches, I found, used their buildings differently than did nongrowing churches. For example, they held multiple worship services and Sunday schools. They had learned that they could not build big enough to continue a single service and still keep their growing edge. They used space for multiple purposes throughout the week—Christian education, fellowship, recreation.

Churches with consistent growth were churches determined to keep their focus on people. To keep that focus, they had left behind some traditional ways of thinking about and using their facilities. As a result, facilities demanded less of their members' time, money, and energy, and those resources were available for meeting people's needs.

I came to see that unbiblical attitudes toward church buildings were among the greatest barriers to ministry and church growth in our time. In contrast to the first-century church that ministered powerfully and grew rapidly without owning buildings, most churches today think they cannot minister or grow without buildings. In contrast to that first-century church that worshiped on the first day of the week in the same space where families lived the other six and a half days, many churches today worship in single-use space that lies unused 160 hours or more a week. This setting apart of "sacred space" for worship only, intended as an expression of reverence, actually hinders the work of God. It shifts the focus of the church as members divert time, money, and energy away from ministering to people so they can build and pay for unnecessary buildings.

After what I had learned, I could no longer champion the sanctuary—space designed for worship only. I began to recommend instead what I call a "ministry center," a large area with a level floor and movable furnishings that can be used not only for corporate worship but also for a host of other ministry activities throughout the week. In short, I quit viewing church buildings as sacred space and started seeing them, and designing them, as tools for ministry.

If the church's mission is to minister to people in Christ's name, church buildings can have only one legitimate function: to serve as tools to help church members better fulfill that mission. We can no longer afford to spend hundreds of thousands of dollars on "sacred" but unnecessary buildings that lie vacant 80 or 90 percent of the time. If our focus is truly on people rather than buildings, that reality will shape the kinds of buildings we design, how we use them, how much we spend on them, and how much time, energy, and money we keep free for the real work of the church: meeting people's needs.

4

Three Things Church Buildings Can Never Do

If you had eavesdropped on a phone conversation in my office some years ago, you might have heard something like this:

"I'd like you to come talk to my board about a new building," the pastor said.

"That sounds good," I answered. "What do you need?"

"The people need a challenge. They haven't done anything for years, and a building program will wake them up and unite them behind a cause."

"You're right," I said. "Nothing is more exciting than building."

"There's a lot of money in our church," the pastor went on, "but giving has been going downhill lately. A new building will increase stewardship. If we plan a project for a million dollars, I think that will be enough to really challenge the people. I've decided to hire a professional fund-raiser to raise about a third of that amount through a three-year giving drive. We can borrow the rest."

"Will your regular income cover the payments?" I wanted to know.

"Not yet, but the new building should bring in new people, and the increased giving will cover the payments."

"That's exciting! With that kind of money we can design an award-winning structure that will put your church on the map, one the people of your community will want to attend. What kind of building do you need?"

"Well, we haven't grown for years, so our sanctuary is old and should make a good family life center. That should attract families. So I guess it's logical to build a new sanctuary."

"How many should we plan for?"

"We have around 300 regular attenders, so we should plan for real growth—say 800 to 1,000."

"That should really give your people a vision of the possibilities and motivate them to reach out. When can we start?"

Though I'm not proud of it, I've had many conversations much like this one and passed along the same conventional wisdom I'd heard about building programs from countless pastors and church leaders. I now realize that the "conventional wisdom" includes many fallacies. When a church depends on these fallacies, disappointment and sometimes disaster result. Here are three of the most common and costly of the false expectations I am guilty of having promoted.

False Expectation 1
Building Will Stimulate Growth

When I designed my dream sanctuary for First Church (described in chapter 3), I fully expected the building to attract new people, to increase the church's rate of growth. It was the most architecturally perfect building I had ever designed. The congregation was united behind the building program, and there were no financial problems—nothing in the process to hinder growth. If ever one of my buildings was going to create growth, this one would.

Several years after the building was complete, I charted the church's growth history. Before the building program, the church had been growing at a steady rate of 3 percent a year. After the building program, the church had grown at 3 percent a year.

It was humbling for this architect to finally admit that no church building, however perfectly designed, can make a church grow. The most a building can do is *allow* a church to grow.

In one church of 160, those who "wanted the church to grow" were promoting a plan to relocate to a business district centrally located among the communities the church served. Relocation, they claimed, would make the church grow. "Our church is in an out-of-the-way place," they said. "Our building is full. The basement smells bad and there's nothing we can do about it. And we don't have enough parking."

Actually, none of that was true. They could double their parking capacity simply by paving and marking the parking lot. All the basement needed was a good ventilation system. With creative planning, their building would give the congregation room to double before it needed to build. And their location was actually better than the one proposed for a new building.

It's true that unattractive or inadequate facilities can hinder growth, but in this case church facilities were not the problem; they were an excuse. The real problem was that the church was doing absolutely nothing to grow. They didn't advertise; they didn't have a yellow pages listing; they didn't even follow up on visitors.

Their attitude toward outreach was symbolized by two stern, silent old men who stood guard at the door. Though each wore a "Greeter" badge, they looked more like people you might recruit to frighten children at a Halloween haunted house. When I visited their service, it was not until I greeted the "greeters" that either spoke to me. Though this congregation did not need a new building, some members preferred to promote a building program rather than do the work of outreach that really would bring growth.

False Expectation 2
Building Will Improve Members' Giving to Ministry

The myth that building programs will motivate more giving to ministry is an especially dangerous one, because it often appears to be true. Building programs usually do motivate people to give. Especially at the outset, large sums of money can be raised for a building program. Some members may even increase their giving for the duration of a long-term mortgage. So what's wrong with expecting a building program to increase giving to ministry?

The problem is that building buildings is not the same as ministry. Building buildings is not the work of the church. The work of the church is to meet people's needs. While a building program may motivate people to give more to pay for buildings, seldom is the increased giving enough to cover the cost of the building.

A rapidly growing church in Oklahoma earmarked 5 percent of all its income for local outreach. These funds were invested in various local ministries in which members of the church were involved, including an inner-city ministry, a ministry to pregnant teens, and several other ongoing projects.

When the congregation launched a multimillion-dollar building program, the people gave generously in response. However, when building costs exceeded estimates, the church began looking for places to cut expenses. They abandoned their earmarking of 5 percent of income for local outreach and redirected most of those funds to the building program. While total giving increased, funds directed to meeting the needs of people decreased.

This church's experience tends to be the rule, not the exception. While building may temporarily increase giving, it usually results in less, not more, money available for ministry.

False Expectation 3
Building Will Motivate People to Minister

One of the first churches I worked for as an architect was a congregation of fifty in a small Kansas town. The moment I saw their building I understood why they wanted to build. It was small, dark, and dilapidated. The members were embarrassed to invite their friends. I would have been embarrassed too. If only they had a new, attractive building, the leaders thought, the people would no longer be embarrassed and would reach out to the community.

I helped them design a building that gave them room to grow. It had a bright nursery, attractive Sunday school rooms, and plenty of parking. They built that building and opened the doors.

That was thirty-five years ago. Though the church has grown some, today it still has not outgrown that building. Why? After all, they did a lot of things right. They really did need a building, the building they built was appropriate to the congregation's needs, and the cost of the building was reasonable.

This church's mistake was that they expected a building to motivate people to minister. If during the building program church leaders had established an outreach plan and recruited and trained people so they would be ready to reach out once the building was complete, no doubt the church would have grown.

These three false expectations all have one thing in common: They all assume that buildings can meet nonbuilding needs. To expect church buildings to stimulate growth, inspire healthy stewardship, or motivate outreach is to expect church buildings to do the impossible. Why? Because these are all ministry needs, not building needs, and buildings cannot minister.

If buildings cannot minister, what purpose do they serve? They are *tools for ministry*. A wrench can't repair a faucet, and a word processor can't write a book, but they can help the plumber and the writer do their jobs better. In the same way, an appropriate building—whether borrowed, rented, or owned—can provide space well suited to the ministries it serves. It can help people feel more comfortable and welcomed. It can provide work space and equipment to increase efficiency. It can make the ministries of the church more accessible to the community. It can do all these and more.

But one thing a building can never do: It can never minister. Only people can do that.

5

Our Building Won't Let Us Grow

When I (Eddy) was a boy, I sometimes went to church with my grandmother. For several years she didn't feel free to invite friends and neighbors to church because "we don't have room for them." She would tell me, "I'll be glad when we get our new building so we can start growing again." Sure enough, the church didn't grow until they built.

Several years later, after a new pastor came, the new building got full. But this time, rather than saying they didn't have room to grow, the church added a second service. Same situation, different response. What had been keeping my grandmother's church from growing was not their building; it was how they thought about and used their building.

Many churches, like my grandmother's, conclude that their building is keeping them from growing. Sometimes they are right. An inadequate or unattractive building can keep people away. But many times when a church says "Our building won't let us grow," they have misdiagnosed the problem. The real roadblocks to growth are being overlooked, and the building is getting the blame.

What are these other barriers to growth that are so often overlooked? There are many, but three seem to occur with such frequency that they deserve a closer look. They are (1) lack of intentional outreach, (2) inadequate or inappropriate staffing, and (3) underutilization of facilities for growth.

Barrier 1
Lack of Intentional Outreach

The "build it and they will come" myth is alive and well in many congregations. Typical is the church mentioned in the previous chapter that was considering relocating "because we want to grow," although they had plenty of room to double and were doing nothing to advertise or follow up on visitors. Some people, like them, would rather blame the building— or even pay for a new building—than do the work of intentional outreach.

Probably the single greatest barrier to effective outreach is consumerism. Most people—about 90 percent according to one survey—take part in church primarily to have their needs and their families' needs met, not to be supported and empowered in carrying out the Great Commission. It should not surprise us that people at first come to church to have their needs met, but if the church then fails to challenge them to live for something bigger than themselves, the congregation becomes ingrown.

Another way churches unintentionally promote consumerism is by recruiting almost every available worker to run programs that serve those within the church, leaving members with little time to minister to those outside the church. While ministries of worship and discipleship are essential, these are often not balanced by an equal emphasis on ministries of outreach. If 80 percent or more of a church's ministries are inwardly focused, should it come as any surprise that the church doesn't grow? If a church's growth is stunted due to lack of intentional outreach, the only way to remove this barrier is to become more outwardly focused. No building, however beautiful or functional, can reach out to people. But when intentional outreach becomes a core value of the people of the congregation, over time the church will grow, and the day will come when the church needs more space.

Barrier 2
Inadequate Staffing

A church in Iowa, believing they needed to build to grow, bought a plot of land and erected a sign announcing that it was the future site of the church. Years later they still didn't have the money to build.

Most of the Sunday school rooms were no more than a quarter full. The church had successfully used double services in the past and could easily do so again. Far from being full, this church, with some modest remodeling and utilization changes, had plenty of room to double. In fact, by acquiring more parking and moving the church offices into a nearby house, they would have room to triple their attendance before outgrowing their building. Lack of space wasn't keeping this church from growing.

So what was? The greatest immediate barrier was inadequate staffing. This church, with a staff consisting of a solo pastor and a secretary, was averaging about 175 in attendance. For years attendance had fluctuated between 150 and 190. A decade earlier, though, attendance had regularly run between 200 and 250. What made the difference? More than anything else, it was staffing. During those years when more than 200 were attending, they had a part-time associate staff member in addition to the pastor.

The pastor of this church was stretched way too thin and he knew it. His hands were full just trying to maintain the status quo; he had no time or energy left to lead the congregation in reaching out to the community. This church will continue to fluctuate between 150 and 190 in attendance until they expand their staff. Only then will their staff have the time to move beyond maintenance mode to lead the congregation in reaching out. Building soon would not help this church grow. Rather, building would hinder its growth, because it would use funds urgently needed to remove the real barrier to growth—inadequate staffing.

A church of 650 in Pennsylvania had five full-time pastors and one half-time pastor, yet their growth had slowed to a crawl. Why? They had plenty of pastors, but only one full-time secretary and one quarter-time secretary. All but one of the pastors were doing most of their own clerical work. One associate pastor spent half of his time functioning as office manager, a job better handled by support staff. Though on paper this church had 5.5 pastors, after deducting the time each spent on support staff work, the church had the equivalent of only 3.8 pastors doing pastoral work. Because the church had grown beyond the size that could be handled by a pastoral staff of 3.8, the church's growth had slowed and the pastoral staff was overworked.

The solution in this case was not to hire more pastors but to hire more support staff, starting with a full-time receptionist. A church member also volunteered to serve temporarily as part-time business manager until the church could afford to hire a business manager, further freeing up the pastoral staff.

How Much Staff Is Enough?

How can you tell if your church is understaffed? We use as a rule of thumb a ratio of one pastoral/program staff member for every 150 in average worship attendance, with the provision that staff must be hired ahead of growth. This means, for example, that when a church with a solo pastor reaches or approaches 150 in average worship attendance, it is time to add a second pastoral or program staff member, either part-time or full-time, so the church can continue to grow beyond 150. Depending on the leadership style of the solo pastor, the point at which a second staff member is needed may be anywhere between 125 and 175. A church with two full-time pastoral/program staff members should consider adding a third staff member as the church approaches 300 in attendance, and so on.

Of course, the exact point at which a church needs to add staff will vary depending on several factors. But if a church has stopped growing, one of the first possibilities to explore is whether the congregation needs additional staff to resume its growth.

How much support staff does a church need? The basic guideline we use is that a church needs one full-time support staff person for every two pastoral/program staff members. A church with four full-time pastors or program directors should have two full-time support staff. We modify this ratio for churches where the senior pastor is exceptionally gifted at delegating. Such a senior pastor can make excellent use of a full-time executive secretary devoted exclusively to assisting him or her. Then the two-to-one ratio would still apply to the rest of the staff. So, for example, a pastoral/program staff of four with a gifted delegator as senior pastor would need two and a half support staff—an executive secretary to assist the pastor, and one and a half support team members to assist the other three pastors or directors.

In counting support staff, include administrative assistants, office managers, receptionists, secretaries, and bookkeepers. Do not include custodial or facility management staff, or employees of a church-operated school or child care center. Business managers often don't quite fit into either the pastoral/program staff category or the support staff category. Whether we count them in one category or the other or leave them out of the support staff calculations altogether depends on their job description and how they relate to professional and support staff.

In churches of over 200, understaffing seems to show up most often as a shortage of support staff. Smaller churches are often slow to hire their first secretary/receptionist (trying to get by with only someone to type the bulletin and newsletter) or slow to hire the first associate staff member, with the result that church growth stalls between 125 and 175.

Staffing to Facilitate Growth

Inadequate staffing may be keeping a church from growing even though the ratios look great. This can happen when a church has hired a staff member to fulfill a job description that contributes only minimally to growth.

For example, one Lutheran church, where worship attendance averaged about 225, had two full-time staff—a senior pastor and a youth pastor—but had not grown for some time. Though it may appear that staffing should not have been a hindrance to their growth, in reality it was. The youth group in this church averaged about 50 in attendance. In effect, the senior pastor was carrying the load of pastoring a congregation of 175 (by working 70 hours a week), and the youth pastor was carrying the load of 50.

The pastor wanted to hire as the next professional staff member a director of Christian outreach, an excellent choice, but the church would need to grow to 275 or so before they could support another staff member.

Where was the bottleneck? This church had made an extremely common mistake—assuming that their second professional staff member should be a youth pastor. This tradition, born in the seventies when baby boomers were swelling the ranks of church youth groups, is today inappropriate for all but a few churches.

For a church that has already hired a youth pastor as a second staff member, short of firing him or her, how can a church get around this growth barrier? The pastor and youth pastor of the Lutheran church agreed to a change in the youth pastor's job description. The church would expand the hours of the support staff to provide the youth pastor with secretarial support. They would also shift some of the direct work with youth to volunteer youth sponsors, giving the youth pastor more of a coordinating role. These changes in job description would allow the youth pastor to devote one-third of his time to developing outreach ministries—something for which he had a great passion. In effect, by redefining the youth pastor's duties, the church was able to "hire" a part-time outreach director immediately for the modest investment of what it cost to increase secretarial hours.

Ministers for Hire versus Equippers of Ministers

Some churches are primarily interested in hiring staff to meet their own needs or the needs of their own families. A church operating out of such a consumer mentality may not care a great deal about how much growth potential a new staff position creates. But if a church wants to staff for maximum continuing growth, how does it go about it?

One principle is that any newly created staff position must have the potential of ministering to 150 people (based on average weekly attendance). A church with a youth group of 25 probably doesn't need a professional youth pastor, although it may need to provide secretarial support for the volunteer youth sponsors. In most churches of under 500, adding a traditional minister of music to the staff may increase the quality of the music but it does not have the potential of increasing attendance by 150. (In contrast, in a church with seeker-sensitive, contemporary worship where the worship service is designed as a major outreach tool, adding a minister of public worship whose responsibilities include but extend far beyond music can allow for growth of 150.)

The concepts of specialist and generalist can be useful here. A staff member who ministers to only a narrow segment of the church population (such as youth, children, or senior adults) or who has a narrowly defined function (such as music) is a specialist. A staff member whose ministry is to the congregation as a whole, covering a broad range of functions (such as a senior pastor or associate pastor), is a generalist. Most churches will get the greatest growth potential if the first two or three members of the professional staff are generalists, not specialists.

Perhaps the most important principle, though, in hiring staff is to not hire people to minister to the members but rather to hire people who will equip the members to minister. The consumer church hires people to minister to them. The members of a church with a sense of mission hire staff to equip them to minister. Ephesians 4:11–12 says that God places leaders in the church to "equip the saints for the work of ministry" (NRSV). If we hire pastoral staff not to empower us to minister more effectively but to do ministry for us, we are being unbiblical.

In Wichita a Mennonite church with a solo pastor had grown steadily until it reached about 165 in worship attendance, then attendance had leveled off. They recognized that to resume their growth they needed to add another staff member but they were unsure what kind of staff position to create. Because about half of the congregation consisted of children and youth, some members wanted to hire a director of Christian education to direct the existing ministries to children and youth. That certainly would have allowed the church to grow again.

But the volunteers administering the Sunday school and other ministries to children and youth were doing an excellent job and were not feeling burdened. Applying the principle of hiring staff to equip members to minister rather than to just provide services to the members, this church decided to hire a director of ministry development who would equip members of the church to be more effective in their ministries. This would include encouraging the birthing of grassroots ministry teams to carry out creative new ministries to people both within and outside the congregation. This person would also equip and guide the members who ministered to youth and children to enhance their effectiveness, but the staff person would not take over the work already being done with excellence by others.

By hiring an equipper of ministers rather than someone to run existing ministries, this church will gain more growth potential from the addition of this staff position. More important, the members of this church will be more fully empowered for ministry.

For examples of job descriptions for part-time and full-time staff positions that equip members for ministry, see appendix B.

Barrier 3
Underutilization of Facilities

When a church thinks it is out of room, it usually still has a lot of underused space. My grandmother's church, for example, was full but it was only full during a couple of time slots each week. When a church realizes it has empty space in other time slots, it can "find" more space simply by adding another worship service or session of Sunday school or by coming up with new scheduling options for other activities.

Libraries, balconies, sanctuaries, choir lofts, offices, reception areas, sewing rooms, and fellowship halls are not always suitable for classes, but often they are. Sometimes a simple change will make an unsuitable space workable. For example, one church had tried using their large secretarial office as a classroom, but the interruptions of Sunday school teachers coming in to use the copier proved too disruptive. The solution? Move the copier, which was on wheels, to the next office during the Sunday school hour.

I have yet to work with a church that could not come up with significant room for growth through improving utilization of their space. Sometimes these utilization changes need to be combined with remodeling or modest additions to enable all aspects of the church's life to grow in tandem, but rarely is a church building as full as it first appears to those who have grown accustomed to using it one particular way.

The next section of this book, "The Principle of Use," describes in detail how a church can change how they think about and use their facilities to free up far more room for growth than they ever imagined possible.

The Motivation Test

Why Do You Want to Build?

Which of the following reasons to build are motivating your church's leaders to consider building? Check those that apply.

___ 1. A new building will attract new people to the church.
___ 2. Members will be more motivated to reach out to others once we have a new building.
___ 3. Our new building will inspire people to worship.
___ 4. A building program will involve more people in the work of the church.
___ 5. A building program will motivate our people to give more generously to the work of the church.
___ 6. A building program will unify our people behind a significant challenge.
___ 7. A new building will make a statement to the community about our church's importance.
___ 8. Our people will take greater pride in their church when the new building is complete.
___ 9. A new facility will provide our people with a more effective tool for ministry.

Interpreting Your Answers

All nine of these reasons for building are common, but most are not adequate reasons to build. Statements 1 through 3 express the expectation that the building will minister. Attracting new people to the church, motivating members to reach out, and inspiring worship are all important goals for the church, but they are all ministry goals. Buildings don't minister; people do. No building can meet these nonbuilding needs.

Statements 4 through 6 are based on the assumption that building buildings is the work of the church, or at least an integral part of the church's work; therefore, when people unite behind a building program by giving their time, money, or energy to it, they are doing the work of the church. However, this common attitude is simply unbiblical. Building buildings is not the work of the church; the church's work is to minister to people in Christ's name. When a church builds for any of these reasons, building buildings has become an unfortunate substitute for the real work of the church.

Statements 7 and 8 express worldly values that often creep into the church without our noticing. The notion that bigger and better buildings are symbols of prestige or success is unworthy of a church that is called to reject materialism and be a servant people.

Statement 9, building to provide church members with a more effective tool for ministry, is the only motivation for building consistent with the church's purpose. If the church regards buildings as tools and nothing more, this will guide the decision not only of *whether* to build but *how* to build. A building designed to serve will look much different from one designed to impress.

If you checked any of the first eight statements, your church needs to further clarify its motives for building before it moves ahead. To fail to do so will almost certainly bring disappointing results.

If you checked only statement 9, congratulations! You have passed the motivation test. But that does not necessarily mean you should build. You also need to determine whether a major building program is the best way to meet your space needs and whether your church is financially ready to build. The next two sections of the book will help you answer those questions.

The Principle of Use

*A church needs more space only when
it is fully using the space it already has.*

6

Seven Ways to Avoid Costly Building Mistakes

"You can see our problem," the pastor said, motioning toward the empty pews. "This auditorium seats 400; we seldom hit 150. Sunday mornings this place feels almost as empty as it does right now. Our little group rattling around in here week after week gets to be depressing. I'm convinced it's keeping us from growing. We'd like you to recommend a way to remodel this sanctuary to make it smaller, warmer, more comfortable. Then maybe we can grow."

How had this situation come about? Twenty years earlier the leaders of this Oklahoma City church had said, "If we build a big sanctuary, people will come to fill it." They had built the building, but the people had not come.

I (Ray) could have drawn up plans for corrective remodeling, but the church, still saddled with debt from that earlier building, could not afford it. Because they expected the building to generate growth, they had built too big too soon.

Another church in New York State faced the opposite problem. Innovative ministries to teens and young adults had attracted new people. Every Sunday saw double worship services and Sunday school, with classes spilling over into a house, the parsonage, and the restaurant next door. Their full-to-overflowing buildings testified to the excitement of belonging to this church family.

But their growth had bumped against the limits of their space. With no more room, growth had stopped. Not only were they crowded, but one building—the one the teens used—was leaky, poorly heated, and structurally unsafe. This church faced the problem of too little too late.

Building too big too soon and building too little too late are both costly mistakes, but both can be avoided. In my consulting work I recommend that churches follow seven steps to plan their buildings wisely.

1. Know Your Community

A church in a bedroom community near San Francisco was considering whether to build. When I asked what future ministries they envisioned, they mentioned, among other things, a ministry to the poor, perhaps a soup kitchen or clothing closet. But when the pastor checked the local demographics, he found that almost no poor families lived in the neighborhood. Instead, the church's neighborhood attracted upper-income families. His people, this pastor realized, were fantasizing about ministry to a group not even present in their community.

The pastor believed that to reach their neighborhood they needed a building appropriate to their changing surroundings. Their older, poorly maintained facility with an amateurish sign tacked to its side hardly looked inviting to their upwardly mobile neighbors. I suspected the pastor was right when, as I spoke to the congregation, mice scampered across the platform and ran beneath the pews in front of me.

This congregation awoke to what they needed to do and did it. The last I heard they were getting ready for a neighborhood get-acquainted party to introduce themselves to their "future members." For the occasion they planned to raise a big, brightly colored tent on the site where their new building would soon appear.

Before your church can tailor its ministries and facilities to those it hopes to reach, you must get to know the needs of your community.

2. Evaluate Current and Long-Term Needs

To find out how well current facilities serve a church's ministries, I recommend an effectiveness review. Write down on the floor plan of your building what happens in each room during the various hours of the week. Then identify anything needed to improve each ministry's effectiveness. Does it need new leadership? Additional training or support for leaders? More money?

Since facilities often are blamed for nonfacility needs, it is important to identify nonfacility needs first. For example, to try to revitalize the church's ministry to teens by building or remodeling a meeting space is pointless if the fundamental problem with that ministry is unqualified leadership.

Once nonfacility needs have been separated from facility needs, the next step is to create an itemized list of space needs, both immediate and long-term. For each ministry, include how much space is needed and what kind of facility would work best.

Sometimes defining facility needs involves more than determining the amount and kind of space needed. A church near New York City had a major ministry to the poor, the homeless, and runaway teens. Even with two services they had outgrown their sanctuary, so they bought land to build. On further reflection, though, they realized that relocation would separate them from the very people to whom they ministered. While they needed more space, the *location* of that space was critical. They sold the new land and used the money to remodel their worship space. By fully using space in two adjacent houses and a commercial building, they were able to expand in the same location.

The process of itemizing current and long-term facility needs is valuable to any church. For the church that is considering major remodeling or new construction, this step must be completed before an architect can draw up appropriate plans. For churches that consider building and for those that do not, this process lays the groundwork for using present space more effectively. (For step-by-step instructions for writing a program of needs, see appendix A.)

3. Use Present Facilities to the Maximum

Once a church has clearly defined its space needs, it is ready to find ways to meet those needs. That search should always begin at the same place: the church's present buildings. Churches that think they are running out of room often are surprised to learn that they can double or triple in size without a major building program simply by changing how they think about and use their present space. Until a church fully utilizes its existing building, a need for more space does not exist. Following are some ways to solve space problems without new facilities.

> *Move groups to the right size rooms.* Many churches have at least one little class in a big room and one big class in a little room.
>
> *Change the group size to fit the room.* When a group outgrows its room, sometimes it works to divide the class. If

a church has small classes in big rooms, a teaching method that combines classes may solve the problem. Large-group team teaching may make better use of space *and* improve learning. Some children's classes can grow in the same room with the addition of an assistant teacher or workers.

Change furniture. You can increase worship seating as much as 20 percent by replacing pews with individual seating. If that seating is movable, the space also becomes available for multiple use.

A room that uses appropriate tables and chairs can hold twice as many people as one filled with overstuffed furniture. For preschool or kindergarten classes, the solution may be to get rid of the furniture and have the children sit on a carpeted floor for their activities. Oversize play equipment—such as a slide—may waste space. If full-size cribs are eating up needed nursery space, replace them with half-size or stacked cribs.

Find new uses for any space not already fully used. One of the first places to look is the worship area. A church in western Pennsylvania with excess worship seating removed several back rows and installed room dividers, carving out needed space for a foyer, a fellowship area, and a Sunday school class.

A foyer can be ideal for receptions, board meetings, or Sunday school class dinners. Some churches use folding walls to divide large foyers for Sunday school space, then open them back up before people arrive for worship. The foyer of one church in Kansas City doubles as an office reception area; along one wall—in space not otherwise used—they've installed six staff and secretarial modules.

Consider what minor remodeling can do. Can you increase usable space by taking a wall out? Putting a wall in? Installing a folding wall across part of the foyer? Enclosing a hallway with a folding wall?

Build or rent a storage building. If you now use potential meeting rooms for storage, this is an inexpensive way to free up space in a hurry.

Use creative scheduling. At one church a children's ministry brought in scores of children from the community. Because they met on Saturday, they could use the only space big enough to hold the group: the worship area.

In addition to multiple Sunday services and Sunday school sessions, how about an additional worship service on a weeknight? One church has a Monday evening "Sunday school." Not only is this good stewardship, it also ministers to those who can't come on Sundays.

4. Use Off-Campus Space

Almost every community has meeting space churches may use, often just for the asking: homes, motel party rooms, schools, lodge halls, community rooms in banks or apartment complexes. Young-singles classes often work better in restaurants than in church buildings. Some people who are uncomfortable coming to a church building will gladly participate in groups that meet elsewhere. Chapter 11 describes several creative ways to use off-campus space for ministry activities.

5. Consider a Modest Addition

A Massachusetts congregation started holding double worship services, but a lot of people were unhappy with the arrangement because they couldn't visit with friends who attended the other service. Recognizing the importance of such fellowship, the church made two changes. First, they extended the period between services to thirty minutes to give worshipers leaving the first service time to visit with those arriving for the second; and, second, they built a larger foyer to provide a place to visit. While neither change by itself would have done the job, providing both time and space for fellowship solved the problem.

A modest addition may also be called for when multiple staff work in a building originally designed with office space for only one pastor. When professional and support staff offices are scattered, teamwork suffers and the staff is less accessible to the public. While some congregations can create a centralized administrative complex by remodeling, others will need to consider an addition.

6. Repair and Redecorate

A church building should feel warm, pleasant, and comfortable. In a word, it should look loved. When a new pastor came to a church in upstate New York, he found a badly neglected building. Years before, the congregation had realized they needed to relocate and had bought land elsewhere. They then quit spending money to maintain their old building. Partly because of the unloved appearance of the church building, the congregation had stopped growing. But until the congregation grew, it would not be able to afford to build.

This pastor, then, was able to challenge the people to repair and redecorate their old building as a necessary step toward resuming their growth. They cleaned out junk, replaced outdated signs on classroom doors, put new furniture in the nursery, and fixed the plumbing. Once again, their building looks loved. It no longer stands in the way of growth.

7. Seek Creative Parking Solutions

When one church needed more parking, a doctor in the church offered the parking lot at his clinic two blocks away. The church leaders agreed to park there to free parking space at the church.

A church near Philadelphia uses stacked parking. Members volunteer to park bumper-to-bumper at the back of the lot and they wait patiently when it's time to go home. This leaves the most convenient parking for visitors.

Can you use the school parking lot across the street? The shopping center down the block? Could you create a "park and ride" center a half mile away, with the church providing a shuttle bus? Most parking problems, however stubborn they may at first appear, have solutions.

While all these solutions to parking problems have been used successfully, several of them also create inconvenience for church members. It's the same with some of the other suggested space solutions, such as multiple use of space, movable furnishings, use of off-campus meeting space, and meeting at nontraditional times. I've discovered that a distinguishing mark of practically every growing church is that the people of the church are willing to be inconvenienced for the work of the church. When church members will not volunteer for some inconveniences, the church is unlikely to grow.

Solomon wrote: "Any enterprise is built by wise planning, becomes strong through common sense, and profits wonderfully by keeping abreast of the facts" (Prov. 24:3–4 LB). The seven suggestions in this chapter are no magic formula. They simply represent wise planning, common sense, and a way to keep abreast of the facts. Churches that apply them can avoid the most common and costly building mistakes.

A church that keeps current on suggestions 1 and 2 will not be taken by surprise when it needs to build. A church that makes full use of its present space (suggestions 3 through 7) will not rush into an unnecessary building program.

By following these seven suggestions, a church can avoid either building too little too late or too big too soon, and can instead build just the right building at just the right time.

7

Remodeling for Growth

Every year thousands of congregations build new buildings when they could have met their space needs equally well through remodeling, and for a fraction of the cost in time, money, and energy. Not only is remodeling often more economical, it also preserves. When we remodel, we use what we have, which has an impact on the whole chain of environmental preservation and sets a positive example in our communities to avoid waste and preserve creation.

While remodeling often offers the best solution to a church's space needs, the process can also be complicated by many possible pitfalls, some unique to remodeling. The following case study illustrates how a congregation can use a planning process, much like the seven suggestions in chapter 6, to shape a major program of remodeling.

When the director of children's ministries at First Christian Church in Columbus, Indiana, proposed removing the walls around two small rooms to create a large, open nursery area, she ran into resistance. Though the building was fifty years old, no wall had ever been removed.

The reason was easy to understand. When the congregation decided to build in the late 1930s, they interviewed two of the most prominent architects in the country—Frank Lloyd Wright and Eliel Saarinen. The building committee commissioned Eliel Saarinen to design a building of a new style, "not a dead style of an alien culture" but one consistent with the contemporary culture of the community. The result was a building famous for its innovative design, years ahead of its time. None of the local church leaders dared trust their own judgment when it came to tinkering with the work of an architectural great.

This children's director was faced with the most basic of tensions in remodeling: the need to simultaneously change and preserve—to update the building to serve the needs of a growing congregation and changing community and at the same time preserve the architectural integrity of the original design. To address these concerns, she prepared a carefully researched proposal and presented it to the church leadership, who then authorized the proposed remodeling.

The leaders of First Christian Church recognized, however, that in knocking out a couple of walls they had barely scratched the surface. They were expecting growth, planning for growth, making major changes in leadership roles within the congregation specifically to stimulate growth. But their facility was not ready to handle growth. To find a way to correct this, the church created a long-range facility-planning committee. While no two churches can follow the same remodeling plan, the basic *process* of planning for remodeling is the same for any church, whether large or small, whether the existing building is a historic landmark or an architectural embarrassment.

Here, then, using the experience of First Christian to illustrate, are five steps your church can take to develop and implement a master remodeling plan uniquely suited to your congregation's needs.

1. Identify Maintenance and Modernization Needs

Fire and safety codes have changed since your facility was built. Has your building kept pace with those changes? Is your building accessible to the physically handicapped? Do you have an adequate security system? What is the condition of the basic systems of the building—electrical wiring, plumbing, heating/ventilation/air conditioning? Are these systems cost-effective? How much longer can they last?

Is your building properly insulated to meet current energy conservation requirements? Have any structural problems appeared? Does the building leak moisture through the roof or walls? To survey these needs, you may need professional assistance.

While First Christian's building complied with all safety codes when it was built, today's codes require more fire-safe exits and panic hardware on exterior doors. Making the building accessible to the handicapped will mean building a ramp to the first floor, adding an elevator that connects all three floors, and installing toilet facilities to meet their needs.

The building has no security system but needs one. The electrical wiring met codes when it was built, but today the main service panel is so antiquated it can't even be worked on. The heating, ventilation, and air conditioning system is no longer cost-efficient and needs to be totally replaced. First Christian faces major expenses in bringing its existing facility up to present building standards.

It may not be all that exciting to spend money, or raise money, for something as unglamorous as replacing electrical wiring, but all these maintenance and modernization needs belong in your master remodeling plan.

2. Determine Space Needs

The next step is to figure out the short- and long-term space needs for all the church's ministries. Do you have enough worship seating for your present needs? For five years from now? Do you have enough educational space? Is it the right kind of space for your needs? Do you have an adequate fellowship area? Does your administrative area allow all your staff to work together? Does your church have ministries with special facility needs, such as a counseling center, a preschool, recreation or outreach programs? What are the short- and long-term facility needs of each of these ministries? (For a detailed guide to writing such a program of needs, see appendix A.)

While some churches will need to remodel worship space, that's not a problem for First Christian. So well did Saarinen design the worship area that fifty years later it requires nothing more than routine maintenance. What *is* a problem is that two services are held in a space designed for one. For traffic to flow smoothly between multiple services, a large foyer/fellowship space is needed. This will require an addition to the building.

Administrative space is also a problem for First Christian. The original building was not designed for multiple staff. The result is that most offices are scattered throughout the building in rooms not designed for staff work. The church needs an administrative suite immediately to provide adequate office space for a growing staff.

Multiple use of space will provide a short-term solution to this problem. Adjacent to the offices of the pastor and secretary is a large room currently used for adult activities through the week. This room can be converted to an administrative complex by installing dividers that create five work stations for pastoral and support staff. To provide staff with privacy for counseling and other conferences, some of the Sunday school rooms can be refurnished to serve as conference rooms without interference with their use on Sunday.

The adult programs that have used this space can be moved to another large room now used only for children's Sunday school. By refurnishing that area with adjustable-height folding tables and with chairs for both children and adults, the children can use the room on Sundays and the adults during the week. The key to making this work is to use an adjacent room to store projects, equipment, and the furniture not in use at the time.

Meeting long-term space needs for administration, education, and music will require a major addition several years in the future. But the short-term needs can be met by using existing space more creatively. As the facility planning committee's report to the congregation explained: "Our first goal is to fully utilize the present facility, while we plan to accommodate significant long-term growth. There is no need for major alteration or additions to the structure until full utilization of the present facility is realized." That committee understands the principle of use.

To prepare for growth, First Christian must also find a way to park more cars. Eventually the church may want to consider buying more property, but the immediate solution is off-site parking. Within three to five blocks of the church is more than enough public parking to meet the church's needs. By providing shuttle service from those areas, the church can expand its parking for a fraction of the cost of buying expensive downtown property. Some leaders have already volunteered to park off-site to leave the most convenient parking places for visitors.

While your church's space needs are different from First Christian's, the process of planning for space needs will be much the same. Determine space needs, short-term and long-term, for each ministry program. See which needs can be met by more creatively using your present space through such means as holding multiple worship services and multiple Sunday schools, and make multiple use of educational, fellowship, administrative, and worship space. Only when you have determined what your present building will do when fully utilized can you know what additional space you need and which changes need to come first.

3. Draw Up a Master Plan

Your facility master plan should address all your facility needs, from the immediate to the long-term, without sacrificing architectural unity. It may include the following needs:

Catch up on maintenance (such as replacing electrical wiring)
Modernize (such as making it accessible to the handicapped)
Do minor remodeling (such as knocking out walls to make a bigger nursery area)
Make modest additions (such as an enlarged foyer)
Make major additions (such as a three-story complex)

First Christian's master plan includes three additions to its present facility. The first will be an enlarged foyer area to care for the traffic created by double worship services. This addition will incorporate a handicap-access ramp and conveniently located restrooms that include handicap facilities.

The second addition will require a major building program. The main floor of a three-story complex will meet long-term needs for administrative space, doubling the space now available. The upper floor will provide additional space for an extensive music ministry, an area increasingly important for this church. The lower floor will be a multipurpose area with movable walls that can be used for activities such as Sunday school, fellowship, and preschool. It will also serve as a support area for the adjacent sunken outdoor terrace. Now seldom used, this terrace will be improved so it can be used for such activities as weddings, picnics, and receptions. The church's growth will probably make the three-story complex necessary within the next five years.

The third addition will be a two-story complex to meet long-term needs as the church grows and develops new ministries.

The architect's task is to so blend the changes and additions with the original building that most people will think the remodel was part of the original architect's master plan. If your existing building is not a good design, however, you will want to challenge your architect to improve the design of the entire complex in the remodeling process.

At First Christian Church architectural unity will be achieved by matching the brick in the original building, repeating the same decorative details in the brickwork, using the same roof levels on additions as are on the original building, and using the same kinds of supporting columns and overhangs. Even the walkways have unique patterns that will be duplicated.

At the same time, it is not practical or desirable to build today exactly the same kind of building that would have been built fifty years ago. While the new additions should blend in as if they were part of the original master plan, they must also be fully useful today. So, as the consultant at First Christian, I had to ask myself, *If Saarinen were designing this building* today, *how would he do it?*

My answer was that he would use materials that are in common use today and would meet today's code and safety requirements. He would design educational space based on educational concepts now used for a growing, large church like First Christian. Rather than use asphalt tile, which he used fifty years ago, he would use carpet. A professional like Saarinen would know that carpet costs less to maintain and is more beautiful, comfortable, warm, quiet, and available than tile. We know this is the approach Saarinen would take, because it's what he did in his day. He just did it better than most architects.

While preserving architectural unity is important and achievable, it is not possible for the building to remain the same in every detail if it is to be the kind of living structure needed to serve a growing congregation and a changing community.

4. Develop Implementation Plans

If extensive changes are needed, you won't be able to make them all at once. The next step, then, is to set priorities. Where do you begin? The first changes will fall into two categories: (1) changes you can make quickly and economically, and (2) those that address your most pressing needs.

At First Christian, for example, the new administrative area can be created simply by new dividers to create work stations, a few refurnished Sunday school rooms to double as conference rooms, and new chairs and adjustable tables for the educational area. Compared to the cost of building an office complex, these expenses are minor. These changes, both urgent and relatively inexpensive, will be made first.

Another pressing need at First Christian is to make the building safe by bringing it up to present fire and electrical wiring codes. This will be an early priority.

Some changes, however, cost so much that even if they are needed now, they may have to wait. First Christian faces that reality because of having to replace the heating, ventilation, and air conditioning system, which may cost as much as $750,000. The facility committee recommends that the church continue to patch the present system for a few more years until the congregation is able to pay for a new one.

First Christian's three additions to its present facility will be phased in as they are needed and funds become available. The master plan gives priority to those changes that can be made quickly and inexpensively and those that must be made immediately to meet pressing needs. Other changes may have to be postponed based on the church's ability to pay, and yet others will be scheduled for future years to meet long-term needs.

5. Adopt a Financial Plan

The facility committee at First Christian, in their report to the congregation, explained that any facility plan submitted would "be consistent with the *ability* of the congregation to fully fund such a plan." How is the congregation's ability to fund a building project to be measured? There are two key indicators.

First, can the congregation afford to remodel or add on without taking funds away from "people ministries"? If the church cuts back on ministry to people to build a bigger or better facility, it has forgotten its mission. Its priorities have been turned upside down.

Second, is the congregation prepared to pay for the project with little or no debt? The major advantage of remodeling in stages is that the church is better able to pay for the improvements as they are made and so save the interest they would have to pay on a loan. (Chapters 12 through 14 describe in more detail how to develop a financial plan for building or remodeling consistent with these principles.)

First Christian Church's experience is an example of a good plan for remodeling, with one exception: No church should wait fifty years to remodel. Rather, remodeling should be a continual process that results in a "living building" that changes to meet the changing needs of the congregation and community, so that the building is always the most effective ministry tool possible.

8

Is Your Church Open for Business?

Jerry awoke Monday morning with suicide on his mind. He'd been thinking about it for two months. Today he was going to *do* something about it.

He dressed quickly and, leaving the house unlocked, jumped into his car. He'd already picked out the spot—the ten-foot concrete wall at the end of Eighth Street. People will think it's an accident, told himself. Brake failure, they'll say.

Six minutes later he turned onto Eighth Street. Four blocks ahead loomed the wall. Tires squealed and engine roared as he flattened the pedal to the floor. Twenty-five miles an hour . . . 30 . . . 40 . . . 45 . . . two blocks to go.

Just then something caught the corner of Jerry's eye. His foot came up and eased over on the brake. Only slowly did it dawn on Jerry that what he had seen, what had prompted him to lift his foot from the pedal, was a glimpse of the neighborhood church on Ninth Street that his wife and girls had attended before they left him.

A minute later he turned off the engine in front of the church building. Aloud Jerry said, "I don't know if this'll do any good, but I guess it's worth a try. If it doesn't help, well, that wall's not going anywhere."

Jerry tried the front door of the building. It was locked. He walked around to the side. Locked there too. Another door at the back of the building didn't look worth trying. Because of the car in the parking lot and the light on inside, Jerry tried once more; he rattled several windows. No response. "Well, whaddaya know!" He pounded a window with his fist. "Not open for business."

As he walked back toward the front of the building, he noticed the church sign. "I suppose I could at least call the pastor." But when he got to the sign, there was no phone number, and where the pastor's name belonged, he found only the shadow left by the now-removed plastic letters of some former pastor's name. With an oath, Jerry kicked the sign.

Back in his car he turned the key, shifted into reverse, and backed into the street. As he pulled away from the church, his car was headed for Eighth Street.

Barriers to Ministry

While this story is fiction, the situation it illustrates is not. It is not uncommon for someone seeking the church's ministry at a time other than the church's regular worship services to find it "not open for business." Just as a well-designed, wisely used building can be a valuable ministry tool, a poorly designed or improperly used building can erect barriers to ministry.

Take, for example, a church in upstate New York that asked me (Ray) to help them develop a facility plan. To reach the church secretary's office, I had to enter the front door, pass through the auditorium, climb stairs, go through a balcony, and finally open the door into the bell tower. The other offices were equally well hidden. The pastor's office was in the far corner of the sanctuary off the platform. The youth pastor's office was in a windowless room off a dimly lit basement hallway. None of the offices were identified.

The front door was kept locked even during office hours. If someone pushed the door buzzer and the secretary was in—which was less than half the time and not on any particular schedule—she would come down from the bell tower and open the door. Otherwise a person seeking help might never get in, even if the pastors were there.

Not being open for business does not necessarily mean, then, that no one is staffing the church office. It may mean that the door is locked during office hours. Or that the church office entrance is not clearly marked. Or that no emergency telephone number is posted.

When a church uses its building wisely seven days a week and its ministries are easily accessible to the community, then it is open for business. To find out how open for business your church is, answer the following questions.

An "Open for Business" Inventory

To see how open for business your church is, answer the following *yes* or *no* questions.

____ 1. Do you have an outdoor sign that directs people to the church offices?
____ 2. Is the door leading to the office area always unlocked during office hours?
____ 3. Once a person enters the building, is it obvious how to find the offices?
____ 4. Is the hallway leading to the office area well lighted?

___ 5. Are all the offices for professional and support staff in the same area for maximum accessibility to the public?

___ 6. Is your church office open regular hours?

___ 7. Are your office hours posted?

___ 8. Is the pastor normally available at specific hours during the week?

___ 9. Do you have a comfortable waiting area for visitors to your church office?

___ 10. Does the person who answers your phone and receives your visitors, whether paid or volunteer, make each caller and visitor feel like an important person rather than like an interruption?

___ 11. Has the person who answers your phone and receives visitors, whether paid or volunteer, been trained to make referrals for physical, emotional, and spiritual crises?

___ 12. a. Does your church have a yellow pages listing?
      b. If so, does it include a map that shows where the church building is?
      c. Does it list your office hours?

___ 13. Are the pastors' names on the church sign?

___ 14. Is a twenty-four-hour emergency telephone number listed?

___ 15. Does the church phone have an answering service or answering machine that gives after-hours callers a number for emergencies?

___ 16. Do those who cannot attend Sunday services because of work have an opportunity to attend a worship service at an alternate time?

___ 17. Do you offer more than one kind of worship to minister to different segments of your community?

___ 18. Do you have small groups intentionally structured to incorporate new people?

___ 19. Do you run a weekly ad in the church section of your local newspaper?

___ 20. Do you place small but significant advertising in other sections of your local newspaper that tell about specialized ministries of your church (for example, a divorce support group)? Or do you advertise on TV or on radio stations other than Christian stations?

___ 21. Are the foyers of your building designed so people outside can see people inside and so see when you are "open for business"?

Scoring: Count your *yes* responses. Include *yes* responses to 12b and 12c as bonus points.

Score _____

If your church's score is:

  17–21 Your "open" sign is shining bright!

  11–16 You usually are open but have room to improve.

   6–10 Anyone determined enough can probably find you—eventually.

   0–5 Your church may be your town's best-kept secret.

The inventory measures how open for business your church is in these three situations:

Questions 1 through 11 reflect how available you are to *a person not well acquainted with your church who comes to the office seeking help.*

Questions 10 through 15 indicate how well prepared you are to respond to *someone trying to reach you by telephone,* particularly in a crisis.

Questions 16 through 21 suggest how much effort your church makes, beyond the usual worship services, to reach out to *people who might attend public meetings.*

Notice where most of your *yes* and *no* answers fall. To which of these three groups are you most available? Which are you least prepared to serve? Which *no* responses point to ways your church could become more open for business?

Serving People

It was because they wanted to correct problems like these that the upstate New York church asked me to suggest alternatives. After studying their needs, I suggested several changes, not only in use of the facilities but also in design. This particular church converted the parsonage next door to the church building into an administrative center with offices for the secretary and pastors. They installed a handicap ramp, put up a church office sign, posted office hours, and hired a full-time secretary/receptionist.

A few months later the secretary told me, "I'm amazed at how many people both from within and outside the congregation come through this door, people who never came by before. They come to get counseling, request information, share needs. I'm thrilled to get to serve all these people."

What made the difference? They were open for business.

As this church's experience illustrates, being open for business changes not only how a church uses its facilities but in most cases how it designs its facilities. Buildings designed to be open for business make public access, especially access to the church offices, a top priority.

Imagine, if you will, that on a business trip, eager to reach your motel, you drive straight through till 9:00 P.M. You check into your room, then walk to the restaurant next door for your overdue dinner. The parking lot holds a single car, and the dining room is dark. As you reach the door, the manager is leaving. "Can I help you?" he asks.

"I'm hungry," you say. "I've come to eat."

"Oh, I'm sorry," he says. "We're open only on Sundays and Wednesday evenings. Come back then and I'll be glad to feed you."

The church, of course, must feed people not just during two or three publicized time slots each week but any time they are hungry. When your church is accessible to hungry people seven days a week, twenty-four hours a day, then you are open for business.

9

Teaching Old Church Buildings New Tricks

"This building was designed for a congregation of 265," one church member pointed out at a congregational meeting. "The architect told us so. We can't grow any bigger than that in this building." In spite of this gentleman's doubts, this church went on to develop a remodeling and utilization plan that would allow them to grow to 750 with only a modest addition.

Bethel Friends Church in Hugoton, Kansas, was bursting at the seams. Ushers often had to set up extra chairs in the foyer to accommodate overflow worship crowds. The nursery was overcrowded. Every classroom was in use. And the staff was handicapped by an office area with no suitable weekday entrance, no reception/waiting area, an inadequate workroom, and staff offices in different parts of the building.

While at first glance it seemed inevitable that they would have to build, with professional help this church developed a remodeling and utilization plan that includes good solutions to each of these problems and gives the church room to double in attendance—all without adding a single square foot to their facilities.

How is it possible to "teach old church buildings new tricks"—to make them work for congregations far larger than those for which they were originally designed? It is possible because buildings that were designed for single-use can almost always be converted to multiple-use buildings. Single-use spaces, such as sanctuaries, classrooms, and gyms, can be made to work for a variety of ministries all week long. Spaces originally designed for a single session—whether worship or Sunday school—can usually be made to work for multiple sessions.

As they apply the principles described in the previous three chapters, no two churches will come up with the same facility plan. But certain "new tricks" that solve common problems have proven useful to so many churches that your church will probably be able to use one or more of the following creative solutions.

The Full Sunday School Illusion

When they call us, many churches say that their Sunday school space is full or almost full. This usually means that "we have a class in every or almost every available room." I (Eddy) recently walked through the Sunday school of a church that had said their Sunday school space was full. All but two of their classes had room to double or triple in size in their present rooms. But because all the rooms were being used, the people thought their Sunday school space was full.

To completely use their education space, this church will have to make several changes. They will need to buy lightweight folding tables that children's teachers can easily set up or take down during class. They can then use the same space for both floor and table activities rather than using half the room for each. Supply cabinets on the floor will need to be replaced with wall-mounted cabinets. Small classes taught by solo teachers will need to grow into larger team-taught classes.

With changes like these—plus installing folding walls to create more meeting places for teens and adults—this Sunday school will have plenty of room to double. Before that happens, though, this church will be adding a second worship service and a second Sunday school session. Children's classes will actually have room to quadruple before they need more space.

From Solo to Team Teaching

In the church just described, making the transition from solo to team teaching will be simple: as classes grow, they can add another teacher or two. One class, in fact, has already done this. In many churches, though, transitioning from solo teaching to team teaching requires program restructuring; in some it calls for minor or major remodeling.

Olivet Evangelical Free Church in Muskegon, Michigan, was having trouble finding growing room for their Sunday school classes for children and youth. From comparing the square footage of their classroom space with their Sunday school attendance, they knew they should be able to find growing room, but no matter how they arranged classes on the floor plan, they couldn't seem to make it work. They considered adding a new 3,000-square-foot building for the youth, but even that didn't solve the problem.

The breakthrough came when someone suggested removing all their interior basement walls to do away with their small classrooms and creating a few large open areas—one for grades 1–3, one for grades 4–6, and one for the teens. They would reconfigure their small classes into larger team-taught groups meeting in flexible multipurpose space. Each space would have multiple tables or workstations so children could work in smaller groups as appropriate. All the furnishings—

tables, chairs, supply cabinets, dividers—would be portable, with a room for active storage nearby, so the space could also be used for large-group activities, such as recreation.

Melinda, Olivet's director of children's ministries, didn't have to be sold on the advantages of team teaching. She simply hadn't had a facility that would let her do it. Remodeling their basement and switching to team teaching will give Olivet's children's and teens' classes room to grow by 60 to 70 percent without adding on any more classroom space.

Advantages of Team Teaching

What are the advantages of team teaching over solo teaching?

Team teaching empowers every team member to minister out of his or her spiritual gifts. Almost every church has a few people who can make the Bible come alive for children, but I have yet to find a church that has enough master teachers that they can put one in every small class. Some people are great at leading children in singing and worship. Others are gifted at working with crafts or memory work. Some of the most valuable children's workers in the church may not be good at teaching the Bible, leading worship, or doing crafts but they're great at loving kids. Rarely is one person good at all these things, yet we expect solo teachers to do them all. Should we be surprised then when teachers feel overwhelmed or frustrated? In structuring teaching positions this way, we ignore a basic biblical principle—that every member of the body is to minister out of his or her spiritual gifts.

A teaching team can include a master Bible teacher, a worship leader, people to work with crafts and activities, and people who are just great at loving kids. Some team members can wear more than one hat so long as they are gifted in those areas. When every member of the team is ministering out of his or her gifts, ministry is more fun, effective, and rewarding.

Team teaching provides a built-in support system. One of the loneliest jobs in the church is being a solo teacher. Have you ever wondered why there is such high turnover among Sunday school teachers? There are two primary reasons: (1) solo teachers are expected to minister outside their area of giftedness, and (2) solo teachers seldom have a strong built-in support system. Members of a teaching team encourage one another, pray for each other, celebrate with each other, cry with each other, and provide practical help to one another.

Team teaching cuts preparation time. If five classes of six students each are combined into one group of thirty, instead of five teachers getting ready to tell a Bible story, only one teacher needs to prepare the story.

There are different ways to structure a teaching team. One way is for a master teacher to do all the preparation and for the other team members to just show up for the class session. Each of these caregivers can work with one table of children, keeping order and helping with crafts and memory work. It is a lot easier to find people who enjoy working as caregivers than it is to recruit solo teachers.

Another approach is to divide the preparation among the team members—one tells the Bible story, another leads the music and worship time, another prepares a craft, another leads a game or activity. In one class, after an opening time in the large group, the children divided into three groups. Each group went to one of three activity centers, with a different teacher supervising the activity at each center. After ten to fifteen minutes, the children rotated to different centers. Each worker led the same activity three times with a different small group of children.

When asked how they liked this way of teaching, the teachers were emphatic that they much preferred it because it took only a fraction of the preparation time required for solo teaching.

Team teaching makes it easier to find qualified, enthusiastic workers. When people minister out of their gifts, ministry is more fun and rewarding. When workers have teammates, they have built-in support. With less preparation, the work is less likely to feel like a burden. For all these reasons, worker burnout is reduced and turnover is lower. Also, many people not qualified to teach solo *are* qualified to join a team, which enlarges the pool of prospective workers.

With team teaching, you need fewer workers. Consider, for example, a church that averages twenty-four children in grades one through three—a first grade class of four students, and second and third grade classes of ten students each. To have one teacher for every six students, this department needs five teachers (one for grade one, and two each for grades two and three), plus a primary department supervisor—a total of six workers.

By going to a team approach, the work now being done by six workers can be done, and done more effectively, by four. When the twenty-four children are combined into one group, a team of four will provide the needed one to six ratio. Since each team has internal leadership, no separate department supervisor is needed. One church eliminated seven department supervisor positions when it transitioned to team teaching.

Team teaching solves the substitute problem. If one member of a four-person team has to be gone one Sunday, the other three may feel able to carry on without a substitute for one day. Even if they do bring in someone, they probably won't expect him or her to do any advance preparation, making it much easier to line up a substitute.

Even more important is the impact on students. The heart of Christian education isn't the printed curriculum, but the loving relationship between teachers and students through which a Christlike life is modeled. When a solo substitute who does not have a close relationship with the students comes into the class, the greatest value of the Christian education hour is lost. A teaching team guarantees that students will be relating to teachers they know well, even when one team member can't be there.

Team teaching models community and ministry as God intended it. As children watch adults ministering together as a team, they learn more about how God designed the body of Christ to work than they can learn from any Bible lesson on body life. As they watch mature Christians love, support, and forgive each other, they learn what it means to live in Christian community. This teaching by example is some of the most important teaching that will take place in that classroom. And no one, no matter how gifted, can demonstrate body life or Christian community alone.

Broader age-grading can reduce competitiveness. Imagine a class of first-graders. When the teacher calls on students to read, some can read well, others not at all. Unintentionally this may set up comparisons and cause embarrassment, much as in a school where some children are in fast reading groups and others are in slow groups.

Now imagine a larger group where grades one through three are together. When a first-grader struggles with a task, the third-grader sitting next to her helps out. The competitive dynamic is replaced by a mentoring dynamic. A rule of thumb is that when there is at least a two-year difference in age, younger children will look up to the older children as role models, and the older children will enjoy mentoring the younger ones.

Larger groups minimize social isolation. My fifth-grade son once attended a Sunday school class consisting of one other boy and several girls. The other boy so hated being surrounded by girls that he regularly tried to escape to the fourth grade class where there were more boys. He was always forced to return to the fifth grade class. If grades four through six had been meeting together as a large group, this boy would not have felt isolated.

On the other hand, at certain ages—older elementary and middle school—some boys are inclined to show off in the presence of girls. I know of a couple of situations where disruptive (and obnoxious) behavior was eliminated by forming separate groups for boys and girls. But even if a church has separate boys' and girls' classes for junior or middle school children, those classes can be broadly rather than closely graded to make the groups as large as practical.

Team teaching improves quality of ministry. For all these reasons—workers ministering through their gifts, a climate of mutual support, more continuity in relationships with students, the opportunity to model body life and Christian community— team teaching enhances the quality of Christian education.

As a bonus, team teaching saves money on facilities. The most compelling reasons for team teaching are ministry reasons, not facility reasons, but often a church can accommodate 50 to 100 percent more children with team teaching than it can in the same space using small classrooms and solo teaching. For some churches, this requires only a decision to use space differently. Other churches may need to knock out walls between some classrooms. Yet others will need to do major remodeling.

The House Next Door

Growing congregations in older buildings often face challenges with office space. There may not be a welcoming weekday entrance with a comfortable waiting area. There may not be a suite of offices large enough for all the staff to work together. There may not be enough work space for support staff and lay ministers or a suitable conference room or break room. In some cases, the only satisfactory solution is to build new offices, but sometimes a much quicker and less costly option is available.

If the church owns a parsonage or rents a house near the church campus, in many cases an excellent solution is to convert that house into the church office complex. Along with offices, the center may include a conference room that doubles as a classroom and other meeting rooms. Providing a housing allowance for the pastor in lieu of a parsonage is far less hassle—and usually less expensive—than building new offices.

Converting a house to office space normally requires complying with building code and laws related to accessibility for handicapped people. A zoning variance may also be needed.

Though in some cities or neighborhoods it is not possible or practical to convert a house to church offices, where this solution is cost-effective, it can meet needs for expanded administrative space almost overnight and simultaneously free up existing office space for other ministry uses.

The Payoff

These are just a few of the new tricks you can teach old church buildings to multiply their capacity to handle growth. Others, such as adding a fellowship foyer and converting a sanctuary to a multipurpose ministry center, are described elsewhere in this book. The financial benefits of this approach are obvious. Because major construction is postponed, the church buys time to get out of debt and save up cash for future construction. Just by earning interest on the growth fund rather than paying interest on a mortgage, a church can cut construction costs by as much as two-thirds. And since building for multiple use requires fewer square feet, a church may be able to cut its construction costs by a total of 75 percent or even more.

The greatest benefit, though, can't be measured in dollars and cents. When we teach old buildings new tricks, it doesn't just save money; it helps us stay focused on the real work of the church—reaching out in love to hurting people who need the healing and hope only God can give.

10

The Overprogramming Trap

When churches run short on space, one question they seldom ask is, "Are we overprogrammed?" When making facility plans, it's easy to assume that all a church's present programs should continue and even grow. But that can be a costly assumption, not only because it leads to overbuilding, but even more important, because it hurts the quality of ministry.

How do you know if your church is overprogrammed? If every year your church struggles to find workers to fill all the program slots, chances are your basic problem is not too few workers but too many slots to fill. (To evaluate whether your church is overprogrammed, take the self-test following this chapter.)

It is possible to diagnose and correct overprogramming. When you do, the biggest payoff is enhanced effectiveness in your ministries, but you also get a nice bonus—less demand on your present and future facilities—and that can save your church big money, money that can then be used for ministry rather than buildings.

Five Unneeded Classrooms

In itemizing the needs they wanted their facility plan to address, the vision committee of First Presbyterian Church in Warsaw, Indiana, said they wanted five more classrooms so they could expand their adult Sunday school from five classes to ten. Their goal was to involve all the adults in their church in a Sunday school class.

Gus, director of Christian education, explained that lack of space wasn't their only barrier to growing the adult Sunday school. He was also having trouble recruiting teachers, and the adults not attending adult Sunday school showed little interest in starting.

Ron, the associate pastor who oversaw home-based small-group ministries, had run into the same problems—a shortage of leaders and a lack of interest among potential participants.

When asked to name the primary ministry goal of adult Sunday school and small groups, Gus immediately identified "fellowship" as the major purpose of both. Which ministry setting served that ministry purpose more effectively? Without hesitation, Gus said "small groups." These two programs were trying to meet the same need, competing for the same participants, and competing for the same leaders. That explained why both programs had stalled out halfway to their goal.

First Presbyterian decided to make small groups their primary setting for community building and adult discipling. This meant redefining the purpose of adult Sunday school, placing less emphasis on relationship building in class groups and more emphasis on teaching, with short-term electives. While all adults would be encouraged to join a small group for discipling in a context of committed relationships, they would be invited to take elective classes only as they had time

101

and interest—not fifty-two weeks a year. If some adults—particularly older adults—preferred to continue to relate in their Sunday school class as a small group, that would be great. But they wouldn't be expected to also join a weekday small group.

This change in expectations removed the pressure to add classes, which also meant that those five new classrooms on the drawing board wouldn't be needed.

Streamlining Children's Programming

Stillmeadow Church had been in their new building only five years, but during those five years, they had doubled in worship attendance and were hurting for space, especially for children's ministries. With a growing Sunday school, children's church, and full-scale Wednesday night program to staff, Carla, the minister to children, struggled constantly to find enough workers. To staff the three major programs that each served an average of about 150 children a week, Carla needed 91 workers. Or she would have, if 91 people had been able and willing to work every week. Since there weren't that many weekly workers available, she asked people if they would work in a nursery or preschool class once every four to six weeks. Total workers needed for all slots: 187.

When I (Eddy) first talked with Carla, 8 of these positions were vacant, and many of the other 179 positions were being filled by people already overextended with other responsibilities.

When I asked Carla, "Do you have 187 people who feel called to work with children?" she rolled her eyes. If even 91 people had been eager to work with children, she would have never had to resort to chopping up jobs into smaller pieces. Carla knew that some of her volunteers preferred to be involved in other ministries and were helping out with children only because of the "worker shortage." Quite a few were mismatched to their assignments.

Carla and a few others went to work to streamline the children's ministry. After identifying ways existing programs duplicated each other, they developed a plan for blending children's church and the Wednesday night program into a single stronger program held on Wednesday nights. On Sunday mornings, then, rather than having Sunday school during one worship service and children's church during the other, Stillmeadow offered two sessions of Sunday school with half the children coming to each. This schedule wouldn't work for many churches but it worked well with the way Stillmeadow handled their adult worship and Christian education options.

Stillmeadow also changed teaching methods. Small classes with solo teachers were combined to form larger groups of twenty to thirty led by ministry teams.

In restructuring, the 187 positions needed for fully staffing three programs were cut to just 60 needed to staff the two restructured programs. And, of course, every volunteer was working every week, not every four or six weeks, which was wonderful for building strong relationships between children and adults. With only 60 positions to fill, Carla lined up all the workers for the fall programs by June—a first—with every position filled by a person whose heart was in children's ministry. Carla was thrilled.

So was Bud, the senior pastor. Bud wanted the church to have room to keep growing but he wasn't at all eager to launch into another major building program so close on the heels of the last one. This streamlining of the children's programs, together with some modest changes in adult programming, gave the church several more years of growing room without a building program. Even more important, though, pruning their overgrown children's programs made it possible to fully staff those ministries with workers called to and qualified for them, enhancing the quality of their children's ministries.

Scope versus Depth of Ministry

A church that averaged about 450 in worship was best known in its Midwestern community for its superb preschool, which served 250 students. Several classrooms had been built specifically for the preschool—41 feet from front to back—to comply with government requirements for schools. During Sunday school, however, 75 percent or more of the capacity of these rooms went unused since the facility had far more space designed for young children than it needed for Sundays.

The church was considering a major three-story addition, with one story to consist of more preschool classrooms. Like the other preschool rooms, these rooms would have minimal usefulness for other church ministries. In the end, this church decided a single-story addition would better serve their needs. A major piece in their streamlined plan was a decision to cap their preschool enrollment at 250 rather than to expand it indefinitely. While this decision saved the church hundreds of thousands of dollars in construction costs, the decision grew out of a new focus for the preschool ministry.

During its first 12 years, the preschool had grown from 75 students to 250. In launching this ministry, the church had intended to not only offer a valuable service to the community but to also minister to students' families. To some extent this was happening. Several families who had first come into contact with the church through the preschool had been won to Christ and the church. But as the preschool had grown, it had become harder and harder for the director and staff to maintain personal relationships with the children and their parents. The director felt bad that she no longer knew all the students personally.

This church was challenged to build on the excellent ministry they had started, not by continuing to expand its scope but by increasing its depth. How could members of the congregation build caring relationships with parents of students? How could the school staff and church members become more aware of needs in these families' lives and minister to more of these needs?

The preschool director, challenged by this vision, asked the senior pastor if her job description could be changed so she could spend less time with administration and more time helping church members develop ministry relationships with students' families. She believed that the best way to increase the effectiveness of the church's ministry through its preschool was not by making the school as large as possible but by developing more in-depth ministry to students' families.

The Solution to Overprogramming

Overprogramming isn't some diabolical plot. Almost every church program is good, started in response to very real needs. Though churches occasionally start unneeded programs, a far more common problem is that as new ministries are created, the church tries to hang on to all the old ones as well. We are not very good at letting yesterday's programs die with dignity, even if the original reason for the program no longer exists or even if two or more programs are targeting the same need and each inadvertently weakens the other or even if there is no longer anyone called to lead a particular ministry.

Overprogramming cripples the church in several ways. When we have too many slots to fill, we tend to view people as potential slot-fillers. When people serve not because of God's call but because they have been drafted, the quality of ministry suffers. Rather than being energized by doing ministry, workers burn out. And they are robbed of the joy and fruitfulness that come from healthy ministry. And, as we have seen, overprogramming creates pressure to build unneeded buildings.

Call-Driven Ministry

Streamlining ministry isn't just about doing less; it is about doing the right things with passion. Empowerment happens when we replace program-driven ministry with call-driven

105

ministry. In program-driven ministry we start by asking, "How do we fill the slots?" This approach can produce many good matches, especially if the church has a good system for evaluating spiritual gifts and call, but it inevitably leads to some square pegs in round holes. Why? Because the available "pegs" never perfectly match the existing holes.

The starting point for call-driven ministry is not the hole, but the peg. Rather than asking, "What slots do we need to fill?" we ask, "What is God calling you to do?" A person or ministry team guides each member through the process of identifying spiritual gifts, discerning call, and dreaming creatively about ministry possibilities. When a person's call matches an existing ministry opening, the assignment is made. But when a person's call does not match an opening, the square peg isn't forced into a round hole. A job description may be rewritten around the abilities and call of the person—the round hole, in effect, reshaped into a square hole, the ministry redesigned to fit the person.

Or a new call may give birth to a new ministry. As people name what needs God is calling them to touch, they are encouraged to dream. What would they dream of doing if the sky were the limit? Many people have had ministry dreams lying dormant for years but have never dared to speak them because they assume they're impossible. When the church gets into the business of empowering members to obey call and fulfill their ministry dreams, doing church takes on a whole new level of excitement.[1]

In a typical program-driven church, 80 percent or more of the ministry positions are inwardly focused. It seems to take almost every available person just to "keep the church running." As a church becomes more call-driven, a wonderful thing happens: We discover that God is giving people dreams of all kinds of exciting ways to touch people's lives with God's love outside the walls of the church. Leadership Training Network estimates that in a congregation where the laity are fully mobilized, 50 percent of the people will be serving within the church walls and 50 percent will be serving in the community and the world.[2]

This kind of creativity cannot be unleashed so long as the church is just filling slots. But when we ask, "What is God calling you to do?" then create ministry structures around call, impossible dreams come true.

The Key to Streamlining

Call-driven ministry provides the key to optimum streamlining. If God is not calling anyone to do something, maybe it shouldn't be done. But doesn't this approach endanger some existing programs? Indeed, it does. As Elizabeth O'Connor writes, "If the church were true to herself, she would help all her people to discern and be faithful to call. In such an effort, however, institutions probably recognize a threat to their own structures. . . . If church people begin listening to call, those we count on most will likely be off on some wild adventures of their own. Some of the tasks that we have depended on lay persons to do may not get done."[3]

But if we want churches where people live out God's call rather than churches where people fill slots, isn't this exactly what we want to happen? When a call-driven approach to ministry results in unfilled slots, these unfilled slots can show us where we need to streamline.

To begin with, if God isn't calling anyone to provide the key leadership in a ministry, even if many of the "rank and file" positions have been filled, it may be time to let that ministry die with dignity. Called, passionate leadership is essential to dynamic ministry.

When a ministry has strong called leadership but not enough volunteers to fill all the slots, it may be time to rethink strategy. Are there ways to simplify, to sharpen the ministry's focus on doing one or two things extremely well rather than doing several things? Does this program compete with another ministry for the time of participants or for leaders? If so, can the two ministries be combined into a single stronger ministry? Should enrollment of a school, day care ministry, or week-night children's program be capped at a level that does not strain available staff and facilities?

Of course, occasionally an essential role has to be filled temporarily by someone whose primary call lies elsewhere. But if such pinch hitting goes on too long, we need to ask why. Has the church erected conscious or unconscious barriers—expectations about education, social standing, gender, official church membership, and so on—that may discourage or prevent those God is calling from considering the job? Does the job description need to be reshaped around the abilities of a called person? Is the support system for this ministry position inadequate? Does the church need to rethink its whole approach to this ministry? Or could it be that this ministry position is less essential than previously assumed? Just what is God saying through this vacancy?

The Power of Pruning

In the story of the vine and the branches, Jesus says that fruitful branches are pruned. In pruning, what is cut away is not disease or rot, but the healthy growth that bore last year's harvest. Unless last year's growth is pruned, the vine's energy is diluted and its harvest diminished. The vine is pruned so all its life energy can be poured into producing this season's fruit.

Ministry, like the life of the vine, has its seasons. One season of ministry comes to an end and another begins. If the church is to be as fruitful as God wants it to be today, we have to let go of some of the activity that produced fruit during the last season of the church's ministry. This pruning is usually painful, because the loss is real, but its purpose is not to punish; it is to increase fruitfulness.

When we hold on to the structures and activities that produced yesterday's fruit, even though they are no longer as fruitful, we dilute the church's energy. But when we allow the Holy Spirit to prune our ministries by listening to and honoring what God is calling people to do today, in this season of ministry, we avoid spreading the church's resources too thin. We allow the Holy Spirit to focus all the church's energy on what he wants to do now, in this season. This careful attention to the Spirit's leading by listening to the callings of our members is one of the most empowering things any church can do. It is an essential aspect of what it means for us as a church to abide in Christ.

And the result of that, Jesus says, is that we will bear much fruit.

The Programming Test

Is Your Church Overprogrammed?

Answer *yes* or *no* to the following questions.

____ 1. Is it an annual struggle to fill all the teacher/worker slots in your Christian education program?

____ 2. Each year, are some people asked to fill slots more because the jobs need to be done than because the people have a passion for that ministry?

____ 3. Do you have two or more programs or regular services that serve similar purposes (such as children's Christian education, adult discipling, or family worship) that tend to compete with each other for participants' time or for leadership?

____ 4. Does it take 75 percent or more of your available adult workers to fully staff all the ministries within the walls of the church, so that fewer than 25 percent of your people are working primarily in ministries to people outside the church walls?

____ 5. Does your church have meetings, services, or programs that people attend more from habit or duty than because they are life-giving? (Clue: Do some of the old faithful complain about the lack of commitment of those who do not attend?)

___ 6. Are leaders other than paid staff normally allowed (or perhaps even encouraged) to take on more than two ongoing ministry responsibilities—one major and one minor?

___ 7. Has some major new ministry stalled in its development for lack of workers?

___ 8. Have you recently overheard any of your lay leaders say that church meetings and responsibilities are taking more time than they wished?

___ 9. Do you have ministry programs in which it is easier to fill the "rank and file" spots than it is to fill the key leadership roles?

___10. Do you often see signs of worker burnout—people feeling overworked, resigning ministry positions earlier than they had planned to, or saying they need to take a break from ministry?

Bonus 1. Does your church have a system in place to equip every present and new member to identify not only spiritual gifts but also personal call to ministry and to help each one connect with a ministry that matches that call?

Bonus 2. Does your church have in place a system that encourages and supports the birthing of new ministries when members identify calls to ministries not yet in existence?

Bonus 3. In the past year, have you witnessed the birth of at least one new ministry program or ministry team that was not started by a church board or committee, but by a member in response to vision God had given him or her?

Bonus 4. In the past year, has your church deliberately ended at least one ministry program or regular meeting?

Bonus 5. Has your church set a goal of eventually seeing about half of all adult members involved primarily in ministries outside the walls of the church?

Scoring: Score ten points for each *yes* in response to questions 1 through 10. Subtract twenty points for each *yes* in response to the five bonus questions.

Score _____

If your church's score is:

-100	to	0	Wow! A truly empowering church!
10	to	30	On track, but with growing room.
40	to	60	Time to get out the pruning shears.
70	to	100	You need to clarify your church's ministry vision before you'll know where to prune.

Beyond Facility-Based Ministry

One complaint never heard in the New Testament church was, "Our building won't let us grow." The church in Jerusalem grew overnight from about 120 to 3,000 (Acts 2:41). Soon the number of men in the Jerusalem church had grown to about 5,000, so with women and children, the total was up to 15,000 or so (Acts 4:4). After that, "the number of believers greatly increased in Jerusalem" (Acts 6:7). All this explosive growth took place without a single building program.

How did the Jerusalem church manage to grow so quickly even without any buildings? Actually, its lack of buildings was probably one of the secrets to its growth. The Jerusalem believers had two meeting places—the temple courts and homes. The temple courts were public space, which the apostles "borrowed" for large-group worship, teaching, and evangelism. Although the number of believers quickly became too large for all of them to meet at once even in the temple courts, the apostles didn't feel limited to worshiping on Sundays only; they preached daily in the temple courts, so we know they had at least seven services a week, maybe more.

The house churches never ran out of meeting room for an obvious reason: As the believers multiplied, so did the number of homes available for them to meet in. What a simple, elegant solution to the "space problem"! (Actually, it only looks like a problem to us; they didn't know there was any space problem to be solved.)

This exploding congregation never got cramped for space, never had to raise money for a building, and never had to take time and energy away from ministry to build buildings. If the Jerusalem church had tried to build buildings fast enough to accommodate their growth, building programs would soon have taken up most of their time and energy, and the growth of the church probably would have ground to a halt. Plus, rather than it being said of the church that there were no unmet financial needs among its members—one of the most powerful aspects of the church's witness—chances are the needs of the poor and widows would have been assigned to a minor line item in the budget.

The experience of the Jerusalem church demonstrates a powerful truth: We may think a congregation can't grow until the church building has more square feet, but the real limiting factor is not the building; it's how we think about and use the building.

As we saw in chapter 5, one way around the our-building-won't-let-us-grow syndrome is for a church to use its building differently. Holding multiple worship services and Sunday school sessions and remodeling to convert single-use space to multiple-use space can often allow a congregation to grow to three or more times the size for which the building was originally designed.

But intensive use is not the only way to find growing room without building. Another strategy that works well for many churches is to move ministry activities off the main church campus into homes or other borrowed or rented space. This works best when it is approached not as a way to find "overflow" space when the rooms in the church building are full (though this can work well on a limited scale), but rather as a way to enhance specific ministries by strategically locating them where they can be most effective.

Strategic decentralization of your ministries can put you closer to the people you are trying to reach, increase the effectiveness of your staff, and offer ministry in settings that are more comfortable for unchurched people. Barriers to growth can often be removed far less expensively through decentralization than through building. When decentralization can slash facility costs while at the same time enhancing ministry, it is a win-win solution.

As the Jerusalem church shows, there is literally no limit to the extent to which church ministries can be decentralized—moved off the main campus. And decentralization didn't quit working two thousand years ago. Dr. Rick Warren, senior pastor of Saddleback Community Church in Orange County, California, and author of *The Purpose Driven Church,* says he is often asked, "How big can a church grow without a building?" His answer is that he doesn't know, but based on Saddleback's experience, he knows a church can grow to at least 10,000 without having its own building. "A building or lack of building," he says, "should never be allowed to become a barrier to a wave of growth."[1] Rick Warren understands that buildings can't keep churches from growing, but how we think about buildings can.

Let's take a look at some of the creative ways churches today are using "dispersed ministries" to grow their congregations beyond the capacity of their main campuses.

Satellite Worship Services

A church in Kansas City has four worship services, not in one location, but in four locations throughout the metropolitan area. This enables the church to more easily reach people in different parts of the city. All the church's offices are at the main campus, and occasionally all four congregations in this multiple-congregation church worship together to celebrate their unity.

Multiple-congregation churches are becoming more common. With this strategy, all the congregations can benefit from the leadership of a visionary senior pastor and strong leadership team. Because they work as a team, the staff is more effective and the new satellite congregations have access to staff expertise, such as professional counselors and youth pastors, which start-up church plants seldom enjoy. The new congregation is also spared the hassle of creating its own office systems, as the existing office staff can handle bookkeeping and other office management tasks more efficiently than a new church plant could.

Satellite congregations often have significantly less facility expense than if they were stand-alone congregations. Since the main church campus is available for weekday ministries and since such churches may also have small groups or other weekday ministries in homes, satellite congregations have the option of using once-a-week space, such as schools or theaters, for their corporate worship.

If a church's main building looks like a church, the architecture can be a barrier to people who have no church background and to those who have been burned by experiences in the church. One way such churches can make an end run around this architectural barrier to outreach is by holding one or more satellite services in "secular" buildings, buildings where unchurched people feel at home because these buildings are part of their everyday lives. Good options include shopping malls, theaters, community centers, school auditoriums or cafeterias, civic centers, and gymnasiums.

The biggest inconvenience of using once-a-week space is setup and teardown time, but even that is no longer the hassle it once was. Churches can now order custom-designed storage systems that enable them to set up and tear down in a fraction of the time previously needed and that make it easy to transport and store their portable equipment.[2] And when comparing using once-a-week space to owning space, keep in mind that owned space is not hassle-free. It requires maintenance and custodial services. Besides, multiple use of space is standard operating procedure for any growing church that is committed to optimizing use of space. Setup and teardown are normal parts of life for any growing church, even if they own their facility.

The trend to "portable churches"—churches that use once-a-week space as their primary facility—is growing. While in the past churches have usually viewed once-a-week space as temporary, more churches are now seeing it as a cost-effective long-term answer to their space needs.

Small Groups Aren't Just for Grown-Ups

By far the most important location for off-campus ministries is the homes of Christians. Throughout the New Testament, the primary meeting place for churches was homes. When we read about the New Testament church at worship, if we imagine pews and stained glass, pulpit and organ, we're getting the wrong picture. The New Testament church at worship normally consisted of people meeting in a Christian home, eating a meal together, and taking part in participatory worship where all were encouraged to exercise their spiritual gifts.

Larger gatherings, when several house churches in a city came together for corporate worship, are mentioned occasionally in the New Testament, but once the daily meetings in the temple ended, we have no clue as to how often such large-group worship services took place. The regular weekly worship of the church took place not in "sanctuaries," but in hundreds and thousands of homes throughout the Mediterranean world.

People are not discipled primarily by listening to sermons or Sunday school lessons; people are discipled by living in community with other believers who love them and encourage them and pray for them and hold them accountable for obedience to what God is teaching them. This is why some sort of small-group life (which certainly can take place in Sunday school when it is structured for community) must be at the heart of the church's disciple-making.

Recognizing this, more churches are making small-group life, rather than classroom-based Christian education, the heart of their adult discipling strategy. This doesn't mean that these churches never have classes. It does mean that classes tend to focus on such areas as skill training or more academic-type training in Bible knowledge. For the life-transformation of discipling, some form of intentional community life is the more effective setting.

In chapter 10 we saw how First Presbyterian Church in Warsaw, Indiana, decided to make their small groups the heart of their adult discipling ministry. That did not do away with their need for adult Sunday school but it did redefine its focus and limited its need for space, as most of the church's adult discipling ministry would be taking place in homes, not on campus.

While many churches are making home-based small groups the heart of their adult discipling, most of these churches still make classroom-based Christian education their primary strategy for discipling children. But in some places even this is changing.

Have you ever wondered how the church of Acts discipled its children? Sunday school wasn't invented until modern times. Yet somehow the early church passed its faith along to the next generation so effectively that the church's explosive growth continued for several generations.

Years ago, I (Eddy) was co-pastoring an inner-city house church. We struggled constantly with the question of what to do with the kids. We tried several things, but nothing seemed to work well. Then I read Lawrence Richards's book, *Children's Ministry: Nurturing Faith within the Family of God.*[3] For the first time it became real to me that the New Testament church treated their children not as a baby-sitting problem to be solved but as integral to the life of the community. Children were not segregated. They worshiped together with adults and they saw adults sharing their struggles and victories, exercising their spiritual gifts, and giving and receiving forgiveness.

Our house church decided to take the same approach. We redesigned our worship to be intergenerational. Children and adults sang together, prayed together, shared together, learned the Bible together. During the last half of our meeting, the children had their own activities while the adults did the sharing and Bible study that was beyond the kids' level of interest. Once we started treating our children as full members of the community, the "kid problem" was solved. It became the best experience of church either we or our kids have had before or since.

Back then intergenerational small groups were rare. Today more churches are offering intergenerational small groups as one option among several for their small-group ministries or they are making them their primary strategy for children's discipling as well as adult discipling. As a result, training and curricular resources for intergenerational small groups are no longer hard to find.[4]

Colonial Hills Baptist Church in Southaven, Mississippi, was a strong Sunday school church. In the early 1990s rapid growth led to adding a second Sunday school session, then a second worship service. Continued growth led to four Sunday school sessions and three worship services every Sunday morning. The church bought off-campus space and renovated it for adult Sunday school. A Saturday night service and Christian education classes were added, and it became the largest worship service and "Sunday school" of the weekend.

In spite of this church's very creative and intensive use of its space, it wasn't enough. Hurting for space and unable to build fast enough to keep up with the growth, for three years the church grew very little. During this time, a spirit of dissatisfaction and murmuring developed in the congregation.

In late 1993 the pastors retreated to a cabin to seek God's direction for the church. They read the book of Acts several times and asked God to do for Colonial Hills what he had done for the church of Acts.

Six weeks later at a men's retreat, revival broke out. But even during this revival, the Enemy was at work to divide the congregation. The pastors were struck by the fact that even though the Word of God was being preached several times a week and a strong Bible study program was in place, the church as a whole was immature in their ability to respond to problems biblically rather than emotionally. Once again, the pastors sought God's direction. Here, as it appeared in the church's newsletter, is an account of what happened next.

> God revealed to the pastors that the church had to get out of the building and into the homes of the people. Even a casual review of the book of Acts demonstrated that this was the original structure that Jesus established and filled with his Spirit. A survey of churches with the greatest impact in every area of the world revealed a growing return to the church meeting in the homes for edification and in a large group celebration of worship. . . .
>
> Instead of building buildings, the church should be building up people where they live. It was found that the cell church was not bound by space, parking, distance, or finances. It also gave the work of the ministry back to the people rather than to professional staff.

Colonial Hills took the plunge and in April 1994 began its transition to a cell-group structure. Within three years, three-fourths of those who were attending worship were in cell groups. Half of these were children. Sunday school as a discipling tool had been almost totally replaced by intergenerational cell groups. Only a few Sunday school classes, primarily for older adults, continued to meet.

Children's ministry, except for children's worship on Sunday morning, moved out of the Sunday school classrooms and into homes. Children's workers wrote and reproduced curriculum for what they called KidSlot, that part of cell meeting where the children went to another room for their own activities before rejoining the whole group at the end of the evening.

The result of this change in discipling strategy? "The groups were growing more quickly than leaders could be trained. God's anointing was clearly evident by the spiritual growth of the group members and number of people being saved and baptized. . . . Miracles leading to salvation, reconciliation of marriages, financial turnarounds, physical healings, and many others are being seen almost weekly now."

By moving 1,100 people out of classrooms into homes for discipling, Colonial Hills not only adopted a discipling strategy that proved more effective for them, but they also relieved the tremendous pressure on their building. The church newsletter report concludes with these words: "There are many thousands to reach and we can see them beginning to respond. We do not have time or money to wait for buildings to be built. The shoe should never tell the foot how large it can grow."[5]

Certainly not every congregation should follow the example of Colonial Hills in moving Christian education of children from the classroom to home-based small groups. There is much to consider in making such a decision. Before leading the church through such a major transition, the leaders of the church need to be sure of God's leading and they need to receive thorough training in how to transition a church to cells. But the Colonial Hills story does demonstrate some of the potential, both for ministry impact and facility cost-effective-

121

ness, of transitioning from a facility-based approach to discipling adults and children to a dispersed-ministry strategy.

The Semi-Virtual Office

More and more business professionals, rather than driving across town to work, are going to the kitchen for a cup of coffee then walking a few feet to their home office and logging on to the company computer to begin their day. With e-mail, computer networking, cell phones, and fax machines, there is far less need for all the members of a business team to work in the same physical space every day. This reality applies to the church staff as well.

The virtual office has real advantages for the church. It can cut the space needed for administration in the church building. Or, looked at another way, it can make it feasible to add staff without building more offices. It can make church staff work more family-friendly for both professional and support staff by allowing the staff the flexibility of working at home when family needs require their presence. It can make it easier for pastors to get uninterrupted time for prayer and study. Pastors can spend more time in the field while staying in touch with the church office. For all these reasons, it pays for churches to think through what staff can best do at the church office, what they can best do in a home office, and what they can best do in the field and to design and equip their offices accordingly.

While church staff no longer need to be as office-bound as they once were, the church still needs to be open for business. Some churches have taken the virtual office concept to the extreme: They have no church office at all, and when people seeking ministry call the number listed for the church, all they get is a recording. That's hardly welcoming.

But it is possible to strike a healthy balance. Imagine, for example, a church with three staff pastors, a full-time secretary-receptionist, a half-time bookkeeper and graphic designer, and a quarter-time building supervisor.

Here is what a semi-virtual office arrangement for such a church might look like. The office entrance opens onto an inviting reception area with comfortable chairs where office guests are received by the full-time receptionist. A kitchenette along a wall behind the receptionist's desk makes it convenient for the receptionist to offer guests refreshments. Just off the reception area is a workroom where supplies are kept and office machines are used.

The senior pastor has a small private office, primarily for administrative work. Most of his library is in his home office where he studies and prepares sermons away from the interruptions of the telephone and office visitors.

The associate pastor has a small office or work station, depending on whether his job description emphasizes administration or time in the field with people. Another 5' x 5' work station in the reception room is equipped with a computer terminal and phone for lay leaders to use in their ministries. The youth pastor in this church prefers to work from a home office and so has only an in-basket at the church, no office space. A conference room just off the reception area provides space for regular staff meetings, for committee meetings, and for pastoral counseling. Therefore none of the pastors' offices need to accommodate counseling.

The bookkeeper works from a home office. Her computer is networked to the computers at the church so the accounting program can be accessed from either location. If a staff member needs a check quickly, the bookkeeper writes the check from her home office and prints it out on a printer in the church office, where it is signed by authorized staff members.

In this church the bookkeeper is also a graphic designer who edits and lays out the church newsletter. Staff members write their newsletter columns on computer and save them in the appropriate newsletter file, which the graphic designer accesses from her home computer. Members who have information for the newsletter either e-mail it to her, give it to her at church, or call it in. When the layout is finished, the newsletter is printed out at the church office and the receptionist runs copies.

The secretary-receptionist stays in frequent contact with all the pastors by e-mail and cell phone. She also notifies the building supervisor by e-mail or phone of facility needs that arise, such as needed repairs, or weddings, funerals, or other special events for which setup is needed.

Because this staff is only performing those tasks at the church office that are best performed in that setting, much of the staff's work is being done off-campus, which means that less administrative space is needed. At the same time, staff effectiveness is enhanced because they are doing tasks best suited to the home office at home, and they are being encouraged to spend more time with people.

Pastors of visitation, many youth pastors, and most cell church pastors are most effective when they spend most of their time in the field doing visitation, friendship evangelism, discipling, and mentoring of leaders. Because these are not office-based activities, such staff members are usually best served either by a home office or a small office or work station at the church. Their real offices, though, are their cell phone–equipped cars.

A virtual office can also improve quality of life for staff members. A single mom worked thirty hours a week as an administrative assistant for her church. To supplement that part-time income, she did freelance work for a client in the evenings after she put her two boys to bed. The church needed her to work full-time, and she preferred to work full-time for the church rather than having to supplement her church income with the freelance work. But it was important to her to be free to pick up her boys from school and then spend time at home with them. She wasn't interested in staying at the church office till five.

The solution? The church networked her home computer to the church's computer so that after her boys went to bed, she could spend a couple of hours on church work rather than having to work for another client. The church was willing to do this, not only because they needed her skills another ten hours a week, but also because they wanted to tangibly demonstrate their support for this mother's ministry of parenting.

Of course, a dispersed staff brings its own challenges. An undisciplined staff member may not do well with this much independence. And when staff members spend less informal time in the office together, it becomes more important for them to structure regular time together for prayer, planning, visioning, and keeping their personal relationships strong.

Space for Special Events and Recreation

In one church some of the members of the facility planning committee wanted a fellowship hall that would seat about 350 around tables, about three to four times the size of their present fellowship hall. When asked how many times a year their present fellowship hall was inadequate, they said, "Just once a year." Is it really cost-effective for a church to base the size of its fellowship hall on a once-a-year event? For a tiny fraction of what it would cost to build a big fellowship hall, the church could easily rent the nicest banquet hall in town for their special annual dinner.

The same principle applies to special services and programs. For an Easter service where the crowd is expected to exceed the church auditorium's seating capacity, how about renting a gym or sports stadium, in the process making it less intimidating for unchurched people to attend? For the Christmas drama, why not rent the local community theater or the auditorium at a local high school or college, then advertise the drama to the community, enhancing its drawing power as an outreach event? Holding special events off-campus, far from being a liability, can actually make them seem more special and increase their effectiveness.

One church was thinking of building a gym to be used primarily by its youth group on Wednesday evenings. They were at the time renting a grade school gym for $25 a week. I was puzzled. Why would they consider spending $500,000 to build a gym if they already had access to a nearby gym for almost free? What it came down to was that the church wasn't guaranteed access to the grade school gym every Wednesday night. If the school needed it on any given Wednesday, the church would have to give it up that night. That had never happened, but the youth pastor thought it could conceivably happen once or twice a year.

Was it really worth spending a half million dollars for construction plus the ongoing costs of insurance, utilities, maintenance, and custodial care to insure that the youth group would be able to have gym recreation those one or two nights a year? Obviously not. What was at work was a facility-based way of thinking about ministry, an assumption that if it's a ministry of the church, it ought to take place in the church building.

This mind-set is often so strong that even when a perfectly suitable off-campus facility is available for a song or when an off-campus location would enhance a ministry event, we still feel there is something wrong if we can't hold all church ministry events on the church campus.

Come or Go?

What if we turned this way of thinking around? What if we made it a habit to constantly look for ways to get ministry out of the church building and into the community? What about holding vacation Bible school in local parks or in backyards throughout the city? What about putting on concerts outdoors or in a community building rather than at the church building? When the church is hosting a special speaker or showing an evangelistic film, why not do it off-campus, even if it costs a little more, as a way of making those we are seeking to reach feel more comfortable coming? If the church wants to start a food pantry, and the church building is not in a low-income area, wouldn't it make more sense to rent or borrow space in the neighborhood where the people live whom the ministry is designed to serve?

Instead of building a gym to host a church men's basketball league, what if the men of the church signed up to play in the city league, with two or three men from the church signing up for the same team? They would then approach every practice and every game as an opportunity to build relationships with other basketball players who did not know Christ. They would invite these guys out for ice cream or pizza after the games, find out what is going on in their lives, and look for opportunities to serve them in response to their needs. The Christian teammates would pray together for their buddies and be alert for opportunities to share with them the reason for the hope in their lives.

How we view the church campus depends partly on whether we see the church more as a shopping mall or as a deployment center. A shopping mall church offers all kinds of programs and services designed to appeal to a wide variety of needs. People come to the church, then, to get their needs met. This isn't all bad but it has one serious built-in weakness: It tends to produce consumer Christians, Christians who think the main reason for coming to church is to get their needs met.

If we see the church as a deployment center, though, we come together to worship and to be equipped and encouraged for our ministry in the world. Most of the church's ministry takes place not when the church is gathered, but when it is scattered. If we truly understand this, we will no longer feel compelled to keep forever expanding the church's buildings. Rather, we will always be on the lookout for ways to deploy more and more of the church's ministries into the community, relating to those who don't know Christ in their neighborhoods, in their workplaces, on their school campuses, in our homes.

127

There is nothing wrong with "come" ministry strategies—inviting people to come to church. But there are many people who will never respond to that kind of invitation. And that is the most compelling reason for breaking out of facility-based thinking and supplementing our "come" ministry strategies with "go" ministry strategies. If the church is ever going to reach these people, we will have to take the gospel to them.

The Need Test

Do You Need to Build?

Which of the following statements are true for your church? Answer *yes, no,* or *NA* (for "not applicable").

Part 1 Awareness of Needs

____ 1. We know the needs of people in our community.
____ 2. We know which of those needs we are meeting.
____ 3. We know to which additional needs we wish to minister.
____ 4. We have determined our short- and long-term facility needs based on present and projected ministries.

Part 2 Utilization

____ 5. Big groups are in big rooms.
____ 6. Little groups are in little rooms.
____ 7. The teaching methods we use maximize space.
____ 8. No empty spaces are left unused.

___ 9. Seasonal storage has been moved to spaces where it would be impractical for people to meet or work.

___ 10. Furniture is arranged for maximum use of space.

___ 11. Furniture has been changed as needed to maximize space.

___ 12. Every space that can be made multi-use has been made multi-use.

___ 13. A plan for minor remodeling to increase utilization has been or is being implemented.

___ 14. We have multiple worship services.

___ 15. We have multiple education sessions.

___ 16. We have worship services on more than one day a week.

___ 17. We have education sessions on more than one day a week.

___ 18. We have moved off-campus all ministries that can be conducted more effectively off-campus, plus any that can be conducted equally effectively off-campus for less cost.

___ 19. If on-site parking is inadequate, we use adjacent, remote, or stacked parking.

___ 20. If practical in our situation, we have built or planned modest additions to increase the usefulness of our facility (for example, a fellowship foyer or administrative suite).

Interpreting Your Answers

Part 1

If any of your answers to part 1 are *no,* you have more research to do to determine your facility needs. Review chapter 5 for research suggestions. In changing a *no* on question 4 to a *yes,* you may find appendix A, "How to Write a Program of Needs," helpful.

If all your answers in part 1 are *yes,* you have really done your homework!

Part 2

Statements 5 through 10 describe changes that can be made quickly and inexpensively. The changes described in 11 through 13 involve moderate expense. Statements 14 through 17 relate to scheduling. Statements 18 through 20 describe steps that can be taken, short of a new building, as you approach the use limits of your facility. Building an addition (item 20) involves substantial expense, though still far less than that of a new building.

How does this test tell you when you need to build?

First, before you can know if you need to build, you have to know your needs. That means you have to be able to answer *yes* to items 1 through 4.

Second, you need to have implemented all the applicable steps described in items 5 through 13. That means you should have only *yes* and *NA* answers for this section.

Third, you should be able to answer *yes* to at least two of the four scheduling items, numbers 14 to 17.

Finally, you should be able to answer *yes* to any of the last three items (18 through 20) that apply to your situation.

That means if you have more than two *no* answers, or if you have any *no* answers on any items other than 14 through 17, you probably don't need to build yet. Each *no* indicates a possible opportunity to more fully use existing space to provide room for growth. These *no* answers can guide your planning as you seek alternatives to building. Only after you have exercised all these options, changing your *no* answers to *yes* answers, will you need to build. Remember the principle of use: A church needs more space only when it is fully using the space it already has.

A church that has only a few *no* answers and is taking steps that will soon change them to *yes* answers is probably approaching full use of its facilities. If that is your situation, you need to be preparing a master site plan that will tell you how much growth you can accommodate at your present site through full utilization of facilities and additional construction. Relocation is usually the most expensive and least desirable option, a last resort appropriate only when the present site, intensively utilized, does not allow for significant growth. Even in that case, creative alternatives, such as starting satellite congregations, may be considered.

What if your church has passed the motivation test, and has passed, or soon will pass, the need test? Is it time to build? Not necessarily. There is yet one more test—the finances test. No matter how pure its motives, no matter how much it needs to build, a church must not build before it is financially ready. If it does—and many churches do—it usually cripples its ministries, often slows or stops its growth, and may even put the future of the church at risk. The next three chapters illustrate these dangers and show how your church can avoid them by following biblical financial principles.

The Principle of Provision

A church should build only when it can do so within the income God has provided and without using funds needed for the church's present and future ministries to people.

12

Good Intentions Are Not Enough

One of the most exciting jobs I've ever had as an architect was designing the campus for a growing church on the West Coast. A group of men in this church, all successful businessmen with extensive experience in development and all of them spiritual leaders, had put together an unusually creative plan for building on a new site. Rather than just buying land for the church and building the buildings, these businessmen, in partnership with the church, bought land for a large new residential development. The church campus was a carefully planned part of the development, designed to enable the church to provide a variety of services to the community. The concept was strictly state of the art.

Added to this was an innovative method for financing the building. All the profits from the development would go to help pay the costs for land and construction of the church. The existing church building would be sold to pay the balance, and the people would move into their new building debt free, with plenty of money for ministry and growth.

Working with the building committee was a delight. I found among the committee members a strong faith and beautiful spirit. Their vision was not only to build a building but to build the church as well. I would leave our work sessions with my faith encouraged, thankful for the privilege of working with such an inspiring team. You can understand my excitement, then, when the model homes were built, bringing closer the sale of the future homes and the building of the new church campus.

But then an unexpected flaw appeared in what had seemed an otherwise perfect plan: The local economy collapsed. The area had been expanding, and new homes had been selling well. But as the local job supply plummeted, people began to move out of the area. The developers did everything possible to rescue the project, but it was still forced into bankruptcy. All the time the church leaders had put into planning was wasted. All the money the congregation had invested was lost. This creative, exciting plan ended in disaster.

"Lord, how could you let this happen?" I asked. "These people are so sincere and so dedicated to you. Their motives and goals were so right. Why this?"

I walked away from that job with sadness, frustration, and unanswered questions. My grief deepened over the years as I watched the church lose momentum and members, for it spent almost ten years paying the debt on a building it never built.

Eventually I realized what had gone wrong. The church had chosen an unscriptural plan to pay for its building. Rather than rely on the giving of the people, the church had invested in a business enterprise, a business enterprise that was not the work of the church. The motivation was right, but the method was wrong. Good intentions had not been enough. They never are. Whenever the church operates in the world's economic system, it experiences the consequences of that choice. In this case, the church happened to get onto the world's economic roller coaster just before it started a rapid decline.

But suppose the church's timing had been better and the economic roller coaster had continued to climb for a while as the developers had expected it would. What if the church had been able to build debt free and without having to ask the congregation for donations to pay for the building?

That outcome would have created its own problems. The whole plan was based on the prospect of the church's getting something without the people having to pay for it. It was, in effect, a type of get-rich-quick scheme, something Scripture strongly cautions against: "The person who wants to get rich quick will only get into trouble" (Prov. 28:20). Such an approach to the church's work takes ownership away from the people. It undermines their commitment to support the church.

Debt

Investing in business enterprises is only one way the church can substitute a worldly method of funding for a biblical plan of provision. Another far more common way churches fall into this trap is through borrowing.

Scripture does not call borrowing sin, but it does call it slavery: "The rich rules over the poor, and the borrower is the slave of the lender" (Prov. 22:7 NRSV). When a church borrows, the mortgage payment then takes priority over all other financial commitments. The church becomes a slave to the lender, placing itself under an authority other than God's.

Whenever I analyze a church's finances and discover that their financial priorities are out of balance, almost always the culprit is debt. Debt allows us to live beyond our means, to build on our schedule rather than God's. Getting ahead of God can

137

hinder the church's outreach or even so cripple the church's ministry that people are driven away.

A congregation of 250 decided to build a sanctuary to seat 600. The written financial plan the church presented to the lender was based on three stated assumptions. First, it assumed that because of the building program the church would grow and bring in new givers. Second, it assumed that, motivated by the building program, present and future members would increase their per capita giving. Third, it assumed that the prevailing boom economy would continue, and that rapid inflation would enable the congregation to pay back their loan with much cheaper dollars. Based on these highly questionable assumptions, the lender awarded the loan.

Once the building was complete, however, the growth never came. The boom economy went bust. Instead of new people coming to the church, people left, because they did not want to be on a sinking ship. Even with increased giving, those who remained could not make the mortgage payments, and the lending institution foreclosed.

This church's most obvious mistake was to borrow more than the existing congregation could repay. This practice almost always creates debt so heavy that the church's focus changes from ministry to mortgage payments, and that in itself stops church growth, as happened with this church.

But speculative business ventures and borrowing against future growth are not the only ways to endanger a church's future; even conservative borrowing can put a church's ministries at unnecessary risk.

A church in Oregon built a new building, taking care to borrow no more than the existing congregation could repay. Soon after the building was completed, the major industry in town, a lumber mill, shut down. Many church members had to relocate to other communities to find work. Many who remained became dependent on unemployment benefits or were underemployed. For years to come, the church's primary focus became the repayment of debt.

Trusting God's Supply

Since we all live in a credit-driven economy, we may have trouble even imagining any way to finance building other than through debt. But the world's way is not God's way. God tells us to be content with what we have (Heb. 13:5; 1 Tim. 6:6–8). Borrowing is a way to get things sooner than we could without borrowing. It expresses discontent with what God has provided.

God has promised to provide all our needs (Phil. 4:19). When the church borrows to build, it says, perhaps unintentionally, that God cannot be trusted to supply the church's need at the time of the need. Larry Burkett, founder and president of Christian Financial Concepts, puts it this way: "The very act of borrowing is the outer sign of an inner doubt. . . . It does not necessarily represent an overt sin, but it does reflect that a church is willing to accept the *least* financially rather than the *best*. . . . Assuming it is God's will for a church to build, He will supply the resources to do it."[1]

Virgil Vogt recommends prayer as an alternative to borrowing: "If our need or project is legitimate, why can't we simply ask God for the necessary resources and expect to receive them? . . . He is eager and ready to respond. And if we ask, but do not receive, perhaps the project is ill-conceived. Can we take no for an answer and still be content? If we borrow, we withhold from God opportunities to bless us and supply our needs. And sometimes we may deny him the opportunity to say no to a project."[2]

Disadvantages of Church Debt	**Advantages of Church Debt**
1. It's difficult to motivate people to pay debt.	1. Short-term borrowing can be temporarily useful while a church is transitioning from a debt economy to a provision economy.
2. The church assumes all the risks of indebtedness without benefiting from any of the advantages of business debt: appreciation,	

Disadvantages of Church Debt
(cont.)

depreciation, tax advantages, leverage, etc.
3. It gambles the very future of the church on uncertain future events.
4. The church becomes a slave to the lender.
5. Money that should have been spent on ministry is diverted to pay interest.
6. Borrowing allows the church to live beyond its means.
7. Debt tends to destroy our peace.

Advantages of Church Debt
(cont.)

2. On rare occasions borrowing is less expensive than renting.
3. On extremely rare occasions there is no other way to provide adequate meeting space.

When a church borrows, interest substantially increases the cost and can even double the cost of building. For example, for each $100,000 borrowed at 8 percent interest, here is how much interest increases the building costs, depending on the repayment time:

Increase in Building Cost for Each $100,000 Borrowed at 8 Percent*

Term of Loan	Monthly Payment	Total Interest	Increase in Building Cost
10 years	$1,213	$45,560	45%
15 years	$956	$72,080	72%
20 years	$836	$100,640	100%

*Interest rates are for illustrative purposes only. Use current interest rates to calculate your actual costs.

If the church follows the biblical principle of proportional giving, with members basing their giving on a percentage of income, the level of giving will increase at about the same rate as inflation, so there is no need for the church to build sooner out of fear of inflated building costs. Of the factors that may make borrowing advantageous in the business world—appreciation, depreciation, leverage, tax write-offs, "beating" inflation, capital gains advantages, lease or rent income—none apply to the church.

When the church plans ahead and trusts *provision* to be made through God's people, the results can be amazing. The first requirement is to fully utilize available facilities until the provision is made to pay debt, remodel, or build an addition or new building. If instead of making monthly mortgage payments of $1,200 on an 8 percent loan for ten years, a church invests $1,200 a month in a savings account earning 5 percent interest, compounded monthly, the church's "growth fund" will exceed $100,000 in just six years. During those six years, the interest avoided by not borrowing combined with the interest earned on the savings account will total $61,000.

If the church continues to set aside $1,200 a month for the remaining four years that repayment of the loan would have required, this will provide $57,600 for ministry. Or if this money is invested at 5 percent, the church will have $65,000 available for building at the end of the four years.

Provision works! At the end of six years the church can invest $102,000 in a building and have an additional $65,000 for building four years later, or $57,000 for ministry, all for the same cost as a $100,000 ten-year loan.

For simplicity's sake, this example uses constant dollars. In an inflationary economy the savings realized by saving to build for cash would be somewhat less. To keep the saving period from being lengthened by inflation, the church should set aside not a flat dollar amount but a percentage of giving income. This ties the growth fund to inflation, increased giving, and the growth of the church.

While the church must operate within the world's economic system, it does not have to operate by the world's principles.

When a church follows a financial plan based solidly on biblical principles, it is largely insulated from the ups and downs of the economy, and so its work, present and future, is safeguarded.

These principles are no secret. They have been tried. They work. The next chapter shows how one church applied them.

From Debt to Provision

Years ago when I (Ray) began to work with a church, I asked two questions: How long has it been since you built? and, How much is your debt? If they had not built within the last ten years and if they were not in debt, I would scold them.

"What you need to do," I would say, "is have a building program every ten years. Take out a ten-year mortgage. Once it's paid off, start the process all over again." I became an expert not only at helping churches get loans but at telling them the maximum debt they could carry and still stay afloat. While my advice was obviously in the best interest of the architect (me), not to mention the lender, I also sincerely believed it was in the best interest of the church.

I now know that my advice reflected not biblical teaching but the world's values. While borrowing money violates no explicit "Thou shalt not," the Bible does consistently view debt negatively and never as part of God's plan for the church.

Building Debt Free

Many church leaders assume that borrowing to build is inevitable. But churches that have chosen to base their finances on the principle of provision—the confidence that God has promised to provide all the church's needs as the needs arise—have discovered that facility needs can be met without debt and that building debt free greatly reduces the cost of building. This makes more money available for ministry, which in turn often translates into more effective outreach. In fact a church that follows the principle of provision can be in the middle of a major building program—building for cash—and at the same time launch new outreach ministries. A Philadelphia congregation, Fairview Village Church of the Nazarene, shows how.

When the church was organized in 1969 with seventy-five people, they made several good financial decisions. They bought an adequate seventeen-acre site at a reasonable cost in a good location—a rural community destined to become heavily residential. They built a building they could afford for administration, nursery, classrooms, and worship space seating about 250. As the church grew, they added a second unit, a totally multipurpose residential-style building with a meeting hall and kitchen upstairs and classrooms in the walk-out half-basement. The fellowship hall was divided into classrooms by folding walls and was used by the church-operated preschool and elementary school.

By the time they asked me to work with them in 1981, they were desperate for space. The first time I entered the building, I opened the front door to find the floor of the foyer covered with school children on pallets. I made my way to the hall, which was filled with school equipment and furniture and more sleeping children whom I had to step over to reach the office. Without question this church was open for business, but this was a case of the tail wagging the dog; the school was overrunning the church. In fact during school hours the church had no space for its other ministry activities.

On Sunday morning I found the auditorium packed, even with the children worshiping separately from the adults. Parking overflowed onto the field behind the church. Every classroom was full. Clearly this church's space needs had to be addressed at once.

You already know part of what happened next. This church, whose story was introduced in chapter 1, wanted me to design a thousand-seat sanctuary. Before I visited the church, that's what I intended to do. But after studying their finances, I became convinced that a major building program would cripple the church's ministries and stop its rapid growth. Still in debt from their previous building, the congregation simply did not have the funds to take on a major building program without taking money away from present and future ministry to people. Building would have changed the focus of the church.

Financing by Provision

Fortunately the church did not need to build. By applying the principle of use—fully utilizing the present facility before adding more space—the church could postpone building for several years. Step by step, then, here is how Fairview Village applied the principle of use, moved from financing by debt to financing by *provision,* and in the process managed to keep the church's *focus* on ministry to people.

The church met immediate space needs through better utilization of facilities. They went to double worship services. They built a storage shed that let them empty out three Sunday school rooms. Bigger classes were moved to bigger rooms and smaller classes to smaller rooms. Chairs replaced pews, converting the worship area into multi-use space. A barn that had only limited use was remodeled for use by their elementary school, Sunday school, and weeknight activities. These changes, along with a cap on school enrollment that enabled

145

the school to move back into appropriate boundaries, freed up rooms for the church to use on weekdays.

The leaders presented a total financial plan to the congregation. The plan's goal was to get the church out of debt and onto a provision plan that met all the facility and ministry needs of the church.

The people increased their giving to get out of debt. Through increased giving, the congregation became debt free in less than a year, without endangering funding for staff and ministry.

The congregation began to save for the next phase of their facility plan. While they continued to set aside the same percentage of giving income they had been using to retire their debt, the church began to draw up plans for further remodeling and a modest addition.

Since the remodeling was already overdue, the church's goal was to pay cash for half of this building project and make the transition to a provision economy with the next phase. The church called this "almost provision." Seldom is it possible for a church to move from a debt economy to a provision economy in a single step.

The church completed the needed remodeling and a modest addition. Removing the wall between the worship area and foyer increased worship seating from 250 to 300. A large fellowship foyer and an administrative suite were added. The foyer not only facilitated traffic flow and fellowship between worship services but doubled as a meeting room. Church offices just off the foyer made the church more open for business by making the staff more accessible to the public during the week. These changes gave the church room to grow to 600 with double services.

The church continued to set aside the same percentage of income for the building fund. Because the church was setting aside a percentage of giving for the building fund rather than a flat dollar amount, the monthly income to the building fund increased as the church grew and giving increased. Within two years after the completion of the remodeling, the church was once again debt free.

The monthly amount that had been going to pay debt then went into the building fund in preparation for the next phase of the facility plan—a major two-story building scheduled to be built in five years. The lower level would be used for both the elementary school and children's Sunday school. The upper level would be a large multipurpose room with a sound-proof movable wall system that would make it possible to divide the space into rooms of various sizes and configurations for education and fellowship.

The church completed its transition to a "provision" economy. The church grew faster than anticipated, with an average attendance of 850 by 1989, so a third service was added and the next building was built sooner than planned. Of the $1.2 million construction cost, $850,000 was on hand when construction began, and the rest was raised during construction, which enabled the church to complete this major building program debt free. This was accomplished just eight years after the church had committed itself to live within its income.

With the principle of provision fully implemented, the church can now continue to set aside the same percentage for building. By the time they need the thousand-seat worship area they originally asked me to design, they will be ready to build it too without borrowing.

Ministry and Building at the Same Time

This church's continued rapid growth shows that it is possible to continue to reach out effectively even while building. In fact about the same time their $1.2 million building program was getting underway, the church was offered the use of a building in an adjacent low-income neighborhood. Because the church had so planned their building program that it would take no funds away from ministry, they were financially ready to say yes to this opportunity to launch an exciting new multi-faceted ministry, even as the building was going up.

147

This was possible for two reasons. First, by applying the *principle of use,* over the years the congregation had moved from using most of their space for single use to using almost all their space for multiple uses. As a result, the number of square feet needed per person had been cut by at least 40 percent, which in turn cut construction costs by that same amount.

Second, by applying the *principle of provision,* living within the income God provided to the church, they were able to eventually pay cash for a major building program and then eliminate all the interest expense which, in this case, would have been about 60 percent of the total construction cost had the church taken out a conventional loan.

In these two ways the church saved over 75 percent of construction costs as compared with traditional single-use construction and debt financing. As a result, the church was able to continue to grow and to expand its outreach even during a major building program.

Almost any growing church that consistently applies the principles of use and provision can achieve similar savings, though the percentage of construction costs saved will vary depending on the church's specific circumstances and the economic climate. If all the churches of North America would fully use existing space before adding more space and would move from debt financing to provision financing, total spending on church construction could be cut by more than half, and many billions of dollars every year would be saved.

As impressive as that would be, elimination of spending for unnecessary buildings will not in itself make much difference in the church's effectiveness. To capitalize on the tremendous opportunity created when it drastically cuts spending for buildings, the church must redirect those funds to the real work of the church—ministering to people's needs. How to do that is the subject of the next chapter.

Turning Church Spending Right Side Up

The best outward indicator of a person's priorities may be how that person spends money. The same is true of churches. How a church spends its money tells what is most important to that church.

When I worked with a Baptist church in Brewster, New York, I discovered guests in many homes: displaced persons, runaways, people in crisis. No one who came to the church needing food was turned away, and a house behind the church provided a night's lodging for those who had nowhere else to stay.

As the church's outreach to homeless people grew, the ministry needed a larger building. Some people in the congregation laid hands on a nearby building that housed a bar and was used by prostitutes. They prayed and claimed the building for the Lord's work. You can guess what happened. The bar closed, the prostitutes moved, and the owner turned the building over to the church.

This congregation's priorities were clear to me, not only because of where they invested their time but also because of how they spent their money.

The Church's Priorities

The New Testament shows us the financial priorities of the early church. Caring for the needy within the Christian community was the church's top financial priority (Acts 2:44–45; 4:32, 34–35; 6:1–6; 2 Cor. 8–9). Giving to the needy outside the community of faith was also essential to New Testament faith (Gal. 6:10; Matt. 25:31–46). Even two centuries after these verses were written, in A.D. 250 the relatively small church at Rome gave regular support to 1,500 distressed persons, probably spending more than 80 percent of the church's income on relief.

Of that period of church history it was written: "Everybody was expected to seek out, street by street, the poorest dwellings of strangers, with the result that the Christians spent more money in the streets than the followers of other religions spent in their temples. . . . What struck and astounded the outside observer the most was the extent to which poverty was overcome in the vicinity of the communities. This was achieved by their voluntary work of love, which had nothing to do with the more or less compulsory social welfare of the state."[1]

The churches also financially supported apostles (1 Cor. 9), and some pastor-teachers may have received limited support, though pastors were not salaried (Gal. 6:6; 1 Tim. 5:18). The financial priorities of the early church, then, were (1) to meet the financial needs of those within the local body, (2) to meet the financial needs of believers in other places, (3) to meet the financial needs of local non-Christians, and (4) to provide financial support for apostles (missionaries) and perhaps some pastoral leaders.

Conspicuous by its absence is mention of money spent on facilities, especially since at that time Jews and followers of other religions spent substantial sums on places of worship. To choose not to build worship facilities flew in the face of society's conventional wisdom.

The Church's Money Today

How do the financial priorities of the New Testament church compare with those of most churches today? A typical North American congregation spends anywhere from 25 to 55 percent of its budget on their facility, including mortgage payments and the maintenance and operation of buildings. Salaries typically require another 30 to 50 percent or more. Then comes giving to various denominational agencies and overseas missions. Usually less than 10 percent is left for the various ministry programs of the local church. It is rare for a church to spend more than 3 percent of its budget for intentional local outreach and to meet the needs of people in its own community. Most churches have little or no money budgeted specifically for benevolence or local outreach of any kind.

While meeting the needs of hurting people within the congregation and in the surrounding community was the top financial priority for the New Testament church, such needs rarely receive more than a token amount in North American church budgets today. In most cases, building and paying for buildings has replaced meeting people's needs as the church's top spending priority.

Ministering Locally

The only way to turn the church's financial priorities right side up again is to sharply cut spending on buildings and sharply increase spending on the needs of people within the congregation and in the local community. While churches also need to give to people far away, it is important not to let check writing become a substitute for personal involvement in the lives of those being helped. One way to keep this from happening is for a congregation always to budget at least as much for local ministries in which church members are personally involved as they do for ministries to people "far away."

Generosity and Growth

The New Testament sets an example not only in spending priorities but also in generosity. After analyzing the finances of many churches of different sizes, in different locations, and of many denominations, I have found a clear relationship between the generosity of congregations and their vitality and growth.

A maintenance church, for example, one that is not growing, can operate on a giving level as low as 3 percent of its members' income. Because it does not grow, that is all it needs. A church with a giving level of 5 to 6 percent will usually have enough funding to support modest growth. For a church to enjoy continuous significant growth, its members will have to give 8 to 10 percent of their income. If the members of a church give 10 percent or more of their income, the church will have enough income to meet all the needs of a growing church, including building needs, provided the facilities are fully utilized as described in chapter 6.

Responding to Needs

As important as generous giving is, and as important as it is to sharply cut building expenses, those two factors alone will not produce effective outreach. The people of the congregation must also have a compassion for hurting people and a vision for how to respond to their needs.

I recommended to a church in Montana that they increase their spending on intentional outreach. One gentleman raised his hand and asked, "If we had more money to spend for intentional outreach, what would we spend it on?" He honestly had no idea. Yet in that town there were thousands of university students, and the church spent not a nickel to reach out to that campus. Next door to the church was a large apartment complex filled with middle-income families, yet no one from that complex attended the church. That congregation's opportunities for intentional outreach were as great as for any church I have ever visited, yet they had no vision for how they could begin to reach out.

That is not unusual. Many churches, especially those that have become accustomed to no growth, have become blind to the needs of the people around them. If they suddenly had 10 or 15 percent of their budgets earmarked for intentional outreach, they would not know what to do with the money. How can a church effectively invest funds in local outreach?

Sunnyside Temple in Waterloo, Iowa, decided to provide a Christian teen nightclub to reach out to the youth of the community. The night I visited the club, it was jammed with teens playing video and other kinds of games. A disc jockey was busy, and the soda fountain was swamped. There were many teens in the corridor and outside just enjoying being together. The Christian teens had been trained to make friends and bring them into the fellowship where they could find a place to belong and learn what it means to follow Jesus. Sunnyside Temple's outreach to teens cost money.

A man in Sturgis, South Dakota, had a burden for teens who were in trouble with the law. Through a ministry he started in the parsonage basement, he introduced them to Christ's forgiveness. The ministry grew and eventually took over the whole parsonage. The pastor had to move to a new home. This ministry to youth cost money.

The basement of the Presbyterian Church in Sligo, Pennsylvania, was filled wall to wall with clothes for all who needed them. This little western Pennsylvania coal mining town was served and the needs of many met. Because it was involved in this and other ministries of outreach, the church was growing. Outreach costs.

A business building next to the Sierra Madre Congregational Church in the Los Angeles area housed an exciting ministry. Trained laypeople from the congregation, supervised by a professional, offered Christian counseling to those who came seeking help. There was a waiting line on evenings the "clinic" was open. This ministry of counseling cost money.

A church in Hayward, California, bought used video games and filled an unused room at the back of the church with them. When the room opened after school, the driveway was filled with kids of all colors, sizes, and ages. There was no charge except for refreshments.

As laughter and play filled the room, suddenly all the machines turned off at the same time. Most of the crowd went into the fellowship hall, sat on the floor, and listened to a message about a new life. Many spiritual needs were met. Parents came to find out what was going on, curious about reports of free fun and fellowship and the changed behavior they saw in their children. This outreach to children and their parents cost money.

"The lay ministers who are going to facilitate the new recovery support groups need training, apprenticeship, and teaching materials, such as the twelve-step curriculum," my pastor said. "We'll have to put that in our budget along with the cost of other outreach tools." Our small but growing congregation of 120 invested in a variety of outreach tools. These included the Chuck Bradley videos produced by Church Growth, Inc., that have challenged our people to reach out; Larry Burkett's workbooks and visual aids for teaching biblical finance; Elmer Towns's materials on reaching the baby boomers; and curriculum to help people identify their spiritual gifts and ministries. Such equipping for outreach is possible because the church budgets for these needs and provides funds for a community-oriented teen outreach and a growing women's ministry. Outreach costs.

Knowing What Needs to Meet

If a congregation truly wants to reach out in compassion to the people around them, and will ask God to show them outreach opportunities, God will open their eyes to a host of needs, far more than they can possibly meet.

This raises the next question: When there are so many needs, and the church cannot respond to them all, how is a congregation to decide where to begin?

A Mennonite church in Newton, Kansas, illustrates one possible approach. Looking for ways to make outreach a higher priority, the members reviewed various needs in the community and considered ways to respond. But as they discussed options, they realized that no one in the congregation had a clear call to lead any of the proposed ministries.

The church decided to go ahead and budget an amount for an undesignated new outreach with its specific use to be determined during the year when the right opportunity arose. Sure enough, several months later a physician in the church felt led to organize a low-cost clinic for the medically underserved. Several other members of the congregation, both health professionals and laypeople, joined the effort. The church then used the funds earlier set aside to help launch the clinic.

An opportunity for the church to further increase its spending for outreach came in November when the treasurer reported that giving from January through November was adequate to cover budgeted expenses for all twelve months of the year. The church then designated all December income for outreach, with the specific uses of those funds to be decided at a church meeting early the following year. This financial surplus was achieved even though the congregation consisted of only about 75 people. How was this possible? According to the pastor, it was because the church was not burdened with the expense of owning a building, but paid only a modest rent.

What does it take to turn church finances right side up? It takes a commitment to sharply reduce spending on buildings through consistently applying the principles of use and provision. It takes generous giving. It takes an awareness of needs in the community and a desire to respond to those needs compassionately. It takes a commitment to designate for benevolence and outreach those funds made available through reduced building expense and increased giving. And it takes the willingness of the people of the church to become personally involved as God directs them to give not only their money but also their time and energy to ministries that reach out to hurting people around them. (For a more thorough explanation of these financial principles, see our book *When Not to Borrow: Unconventional Financial Wisdom to Set Your Church Free.*)

Turning church finances right side up is possible but it is not something that can be accomplished casually. It calls for nothing less than turning the very priorities of the church right side up again.

The Finances Test

Are You Financially Ready to Build?

Which of the following are true for your church? Check those that apply.

___ 1. The regular giving in our church is strong.
___ 2. The giving units—individuals or families who give regularly—represent a majority of the congregation.
___ 3. We consistently meet our budget, fully funding our ministries and staff needs.
___ 4. Our budget includes adequate funds for intentional outreach and for meeting the needs of people in our community.
___ 5. We teach biblical finance for families and individuals, including an emphasis on biblical giving.
___ 6. The church is out of debt.
___ 7. In a survey the present giving units have committed themselves to an increase in their giving to cover the cost of construction and future building operation costs, so that none of the church's present ministry spending will be diverted to building.

____ 8. The increased giving for future facility needs has been invested in an interest-bearing provision fund.

____ 9. The church has invested enough in its provision fund to be able to pay cash or almost cash for the proposed building program.

Interpreting Your Results

If you checked statements 1 through 6, your church is probably basically financially healthy, and by implementing the strategies of 7, 8, and 9, you should be financially ready to build within a few years. When all nine statements are true for your church, you pass the financial readiness test.

You have now studied three principles: the *principle of focus,* the *principle of use,* and the *principle of provision.* You have taken three corresponding tests: the motivation test, the need test, and the finances test. Few, if any, churches will "pass" all three tests the first time they take them. That does not mean such churches do not "measure up." In most cases it means the church does not need to build yet or it needs to do more planning, growing, or saving before it launches a building program.

The results of these three tests, taken together, identify issues the church needs to address and steps the church needs to take in its facility decisions. A growing church that carefully follows these steps will eventually achieve full utilization of its existing facility and become financially prepared to build. When such a church can retake all three tests and "pass" all three, then it is time to build. In fact to delay building beyond that point may hinder the church's growth.

As a church approaches the time to build, it will need to form a church-growth committee to carefully plan what kind of facility can best serve the church in its continued growth and outreach. Chapter 15 tells how to find the right people for that growth committee (they are not who you would think), and chapters 16 and 17 explain how to design a building specifically suited to the needs of the growing congregation.

Even if your church is years away from a major building program, you will find practical ideas in these next three chapters and the appendix that may help you turn your present facility into a more effective ministry tool.

When It's Time to Build

By creatively using its existing facilities, a church can grow to two or three times the size it otherwise could, without a major building program. But if the church continues to grow, the time to build will come. When that time comes, how does the church go about it?

Who Should and Should Not Plan Your Building

When Parkside Church outgrew their building, Pastor Smith considered himself fortunate. Though he had no training or experience in building, the congregation included several professionals in the building trades. So once the congregation voted to move ahead with a new building program, the board had no trouble appointing a building committee consisting primarily of construction professionals.

Paul was a plumber.
Carl was a rough-in carpenter.
Bill built warehouses.
Charlie was an excavator.
Cal was a concrete contractor.
Helen had designed her own house.

Don was a draftsman.

Joy was known for the interior decoration of her home.

The committee was appointed and went to work. Their first task was to design the new building. What rooms were needed? How large should they be? Where should they go? At what stage of the church's growth would each room be needed?

The options became even more complex when they started considering how to use their existing building. Not that there was any shortage of creative ideas; everyone had suggestions. After a dozen meetings, though, the committee was no closer to a decision. It became obvious that they needed to bring in a professional to put this puzzle together.

Fortunately Bill had a good friend, Arch, who was an architect. Arch had recently designed a building for another denomination in town to replace their deteriorating older structure. With a little adaptation, Arch was able to make his "stock plan" fit with Parkside's existing building and give it a striking exterior appearance.

The church hired Bill to be the construction superintendent, and several other committee members became subcontractors. Pastor Smith occasionally mentioned from the pulpit how fortunate the church was to have so many people trained and gifted in building, and how much money it was saving the church.

But before long the committee hit some snags. Poor contractual and payment procedures caused unnecessary expenses. As construction costs escalated, an additional loan became necessary. When construction was finished, the committee found they had no funds left for furnishings, landscaping, or to pave the parking lot. Worse yet, because of the unexpectedly high debt burden, the church had to delay hiring the new associate pastor and could not replace the secretary who had just resigned.

The building had simply cost too much. And it soon became apparent that in spite of its high price, the building was still inadequate. Somehow the congregation's needs for fellow-ship space had been largely overlooked. And many of the rooms were too small to provide for the open room and team teaching approaches needed in the growing Sunday school classes. The problem, Pastor Smith realized in retrospect, was that Arch's plans had been designed for a static church, one that was not growing. As a growing congregation, Parkside needed a different kind of facility.

Why, Pastor Smith wondered, with so many reputable con-struction professionals on the building committee, had they ended up with an overpriced building so poorly suited to the congregation's needs?

Experts in the Church

The answer, surprisingly enough, is to be found in the way the building committee was selected. The story you have just read is not the story of a single church, but rather a compos-ite story of scores of churches. While the specifics vary, this basic approach to putting together a building committee has been followed by at least 80 percent of the churches I have worked with as architect.

Construction Experts

One church in Arkansas, for example, hired me to draw up building plans for them. The building committee included, among others, a cabinetmaker, a plumber, and a small con-tractor. The church ended up with really good cabinets, and the plumbing was excellent, but I was never quite sure the building fit the ministries of the church.

Is it a mistake, then, to rely on construction professionals within the congregation when the church builds? No, not at all. The skills these members bring can be extremely valuable during a building program. The problem arises when con-

165

struction experts are expected to perform functions outside their areas of expertise.

The key to solving this common problem is found in the recognition that planning and construction are two distinct functions that call for two distinct sets of skills. Those best able to supervise construction are the construction experts. Those best able to decide what kind of space is needed to facilitate ministry, however, are not the construction experts but ministry experts—those who actively direct the ministry programs the building will serve.

One church on the East Coast has tried it both ways. In the early 1980s the church made a $200,000 addition to its building. Their building committee was set up the usual way, with a cabinetmaker from the congregation as chairman. The cabinetmaker (let's call him Gary) was a great guy and very well-intentioned but he didn't have the planning skills that a $200,000 building program called for. He was not a "big picture" person. Fortunately the church had hired an outside consultant who was able to guide the committee in the right direction on design decisions, often in spite of Gary.

But even that did not control all the damage. Gary took personal responsibility for a portion of the remodeling. Once he got into it, it became obvious that he was in over his head. The church finally had to hire someone else to come in and finish the job at a higher total cost than if they had hired a professional in the first place. Because Gary was serving outside his area of expertise, the church wasted time and money, and leaders had to resolve some sticky and unnecessary relationship problems.

Ministry Experts

A few years later the church built a million-dollar building. This time, though, the responsibility to plan the new building was given to a growth task force made up of laypeople and church staff who were active ministry leaders.

166

This task force was not so easy to appoint. Great care was taken to select those who could best identify what kinds of facilities the growing church's ministries would need in years to come. The task force included spiritual leaders active in ministries to children, youth, and adults, in the music ministry, in outreach, and in administration. It also included some whose jobs gave them an understanding of the community the church served.

The task force asked all those in the congregation with specialized construction skills to list their credentials. Those who responded became a pool of advisors whose expertise was called on as needed during planning and construction.

In areas where the congregation had no experts, the church employed consultants. Because this church placed high priority on planning, not only did they hire architects and engineers for the construction phase, they also hired a church planning specialist to guide the task force and help them prepare their work in a form useful to the architects and engineers.

FIGURE 4

The Planning and Construction Functions in a Building Program

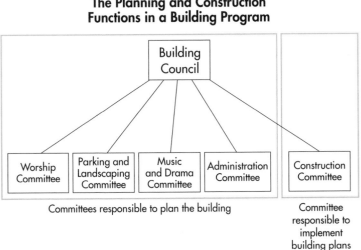

167

Matching Experts and Responsibilities

There is no single right way to separate the planning function from construction. A church in Kansas City achieved the same result with another approach. They created a building council made up of ministry leaders to plan the building. Subcommittees for worship, music and drama, landscape and parking, and administration reported to this council. Each developed proposals in its area of specialty.

The construction experts—plumbers, building contractors, and so on—were not found on either the building council or any of its planning subcommittees. They served instead on another subcommittee called the construction committee. Once the council had defined what kind of facility was needed, it became the construction committee's responsibility to implement those plans by hiring the architects and engineers and overseeing actual construction.

By separating planning and construction functions, this church has involved both ministry experts and construction experts where they can make their greatest contributions without expecting either to make decisions outside their areas of expertise.

The key, then, to putting together an effective building team is the same principle that should guide all aspects of staffing the church's work: Match people's abilities to the corresponding responsibilities. When applied to a building program, the principle works like this:

1. To plan the kind of facilities that can best serve your present and future ministries and to write your program of facility needs (see appendix A), call on your ministry experts. We like to call this group the church-growth committee.
2. To oversee construction of your building, call on your construction experts.

3. For any aspects of your building program, either planning or construction, for which you do not have experts within the congregation, hire outside professionals.

By using this approach in their most recent building, the East Coast church avoided the problems they had had last time. Neither Gary nor any of the other construction specialists experienced the frustration of getting in over their heads, yet they all had opportunity to contribute their expertise. And today the congregation enjoys the use of a versatile building uniquely suited to their full schedule of ministry activities.

16

Designing Your Facilities for Multiple Use

Traditionally church buildings have been designed as single-use facilities. The sanctuary is used for worship, classrooms for Christian education, the fellowship hall for dinners, the gymnasium for recreation. This is how church architects, including me, have been trained to build. For many years that was how I designed buildings and because I worked mostly with nongrowing congregations, that approach served both me and the congregations well.

But once I began to work mostly with growing churches, I ran into a problem: Single-use architecture and continuing growth just don't mix. As today's fastest-growing congregations have discovered, to build single-use buildings fast enough to keep pace with their space needs is usually prohibitively expensive. Even when it is possible, growing churches discover again and again that unnecessary building programs siphon away from the real work of the church the very time, money, and energy that have made its ministries effective and stimulated its growth. When that happens growth usually slows or stops.

To meet the needs of the growing church and preserve its growing edge, a different kind of architecture is needed, one for which most architects have not been trained. The growing church needs not a single-use facility but a multi-use facility—one where almost every space is designed to be used for multiple functions seven days a week.

My work with growing churches has forced me to abandon many of my traditional design ideas and to adopt—often from the churches I work with—designs with innovative multi-use features. Here are the most important of those features.

The Ministry Center

I used to believe that worship services should take place in a sanctuary, a holy place set apart exclusively for the worship of God. In my work with growing churches, though, I discovered that most of them did not have enough space for all their ministries, and if they kept growing, they would probably never have enough. As a consultant, I faced a choice: Either leave the worship space lying unused 90 percent of the time and tell the churches to stop growing, or find a way for these churches to use that space the other six and a half days a week.

The solution that has evolved over the years is what I call a ministry center. This is a meeting space designed for the liturgy of the church: worship, music, baptism, communion, weddings, funerals, and teaching. If the congregation wishes, the ministry center can also accommodate drama, concerts, films, multimedia presentations, and other special programs. Depending on the needs and desires of the congregation, it can also be designed for other ministries throughout the week:

171

fellowship dinners, teens' and children's activities, senior citizens' programs, or school use.

The key to making the ministry center work for a wide variety of uses is movable seating: comfortable church chairs on a flat floor. This makes it possible to tailor the seating to the nature of the service or event. For example, while a center aisle is needed for weddings, side aisles work better for preaching and teaching so more people can be seated in front of the speaker. For funerals the front few rows can be removed and the family seated to one side.

With movable seating more or fewer chairs can be set up, depending on attendance, to avoid the half-empty feeling that can inhibit growth. Chairs can be arranged to form small groups for discussion, sharing, or prayer. Tables may be added for conferences, teaching, or fellowship. Seating can face different directions, be angled, or set up in the round. Continental seating—rows spaced far enough apart to allow easy movement in and out of the rows—is another option.

Chairs also enable more people to be seated in the same space. (Few people will sit on two chairs.) While a pew has room for ten people at twenty-one inches each (a comfortable width for a chair), on the average only eight will sit in the space. In most churches, changing to chairs increases the effective seating capacity by 10 to 20 percent.

A feature that can enhance the versatility of the ministry center is a partly or totally movable platform and movable choir risers. This allows for different sizes of choirs or musical groups and for various arrangements of staging—even in different parts of the room—for drama or orchestras. When there is no choir, the risers can be removed to eliminate the void of an empty choir loft.

Designing a lighting system for this space will require the ability of the best illumination engineer available. You will need equally expert help with acoustics and sound, since the acoustical treatment will have to be designed to work not from one direction but many. The most satisfactory sound system may be the movable "concert" type with several places around the room where controls, speakers, and microphones can be plugged in.

For total flexibility, front or back projection screens can also be movable rather than fixed. Electronic keyboards work better with this concept than a pipe organ (as much as I love pipe organs).

I used to believe that churches could not afford much storage space, because they needed the space for active use. What I've learned from growing churches is that multi-use spaces work well only when there are large storage spaces nearby so furniture, chairs, staging, and equipment can be moved in and out quickly.

While active storage should be adjacent to the room where the equipment is used, seldom used items, such as old files, Christmas decorations, and drama props, can be stored in less accessible space—attics, garages, or storage sheds.

Smaller Capacity

Two or three Sunday services are normal for many growing churches, plus, in some cases, services during the week.

While doing research for my masters degree in church design, I interviewed a Catholic priest. "How do you decide how many services to have and when to have them?" I asked.

He answered, "We have as many as are needed to serve the people, whenever they need them. For example, for people who have to work on Sunday, we have a Saturday mass."

"How many have to attend before you'll schedule a service?" I asked.

His answer: "That's not important. We're here to serve."

When designing a new building, wouldn't it make sense at the same time to plan as many worship services as are needed at the times people need them? Compared with a single-service plan, this would make it possible to build a much smaller ministry center. Not only would this save money, but it would also bring people closer together and go far toward eliminating the problem of a meeting space that feels too big and impersonal. A moderately sized ministry center is also easier to subdivide into smaller meeting spaces than is a large auditorium, and it increases the variety of ministries for which the space can be used.

Just as multiple services make it possible to build a smaller ministry center, multiple sessions for Christian education make it possible to construct far less educational space. But building for high intensity use does not simply mean building smaller. A facility designed for multiple Sunday services and multiple Sunday school sessions has special requirements.

In many churches that hold multiple services and Sunday school sessions, some people will go from worship to Sunday school while others are coming from Sunday school to worship. Some will arrive for the second service while others leave from the first service. This means that entryways and hallways in the multiservice building need to be designed to handle at least twice as much traffic as those in a single-service building. Parking will also need to be expanded with clearly marked entrances, exits, and traffic patterns, and more areas for loading and unloading passengers must be added.

Multiple services create yet one more special demand on a facility. In single-service churches people often linger in the worship area to visit after the service, standing between pews, in aisles, or in the back of the auditorium. A multiple-service church, however, must clear the worship area fairly quickly, so arriving worshipers can enter. In addition, worshipers leaving the first service and those arriving for the second need a place where they can visit with each other. These needs and others can be met by another special feature designed specifically for the multi-use church—a fellowship foyer.

The Fellowship Foyer

The fellowship foyer is a room at least half the size of the ministry center (worship area). Like the traditional foyer, this is where people enter as they arrive for worship and from here they enter the worship area. Unlike a traditional foyer, however, it is large enough to give worshipers leaving one service and those arriving for the next plenty of room to visit with each other and welcome visitors without blocking traffic.

Besides serving as a foyer, this room also fulfills all the functions of the traditional fellowship hall. A small serving kitchen to one side makes it ideal for serving light refreshments or even for banquets and receptions. This space is also well suited for conferences, recreational activities, work projects, and board meetings.

Like other multi-use space, the fellowship foyer needs ample storage for chairs, tables, equipment, and possibly staging. One option is to include movable walls to subdivide the room for use by smaller groups and classes. The fellowship foyer is an extremely versatile space that the people of the church will use almost every time they gather.

Space for Education

In the small church we design classrooms for a single teacher with a small number of students. While little rooms work well when classes are small, as the church grows, rows of little rooms no longer meet the church's educational needs.

A growing church will need multiple nurseries and large open spaces for children's classes that can be subdivided with folding walls, movable dividers, and/or movable supply storage units. It will need a single room large enough to hold the entire teen group. For its adult classes the church may need a few large rooms, many small meeting spaces, or a mixture of large and small spaces. As some classes grow and new ones are formed, the size of the meeting spaces needed is almost sure to keep changing. How can a church plan for such constant change?

The key is flexibility. Design space with movable walls that can be used to create spaces of various sizes. Or design rooms of varying sizes so, for example, as the teen group grows, it can be moved into progressively larger rooms. Another solution to the same problem is to build temporary walls that can be removed to allow for growth and thereby expand the size of the room in stages. (See appendix A for a description of the kind and amount of educational space needed for nursery, children's classes, teens, and adults.)

Making the educational space multi-use means not only that it is used for multiple sessions of Sunday school, but that it is available for a variety of functions all week long, such as a latchkey program and weeknight children's programs. To make weekday utilization practical, include movable, lockable supply cabinets for the workers and big storage rooms for the furniture and equipment that the various programs use. This area also needs a serving kitchen, toilet facilities, and a directly controlled outside entrance that allows it to be used independently from the rest of the building.

Parking and Recreation

Another simple way to achieve multiple use is to use hard-surfaced parking lots for recreation. Space used for parking on Sunday can double as basketball, volleyball, and tennis courts during the week. Paved parking lots are also well suited to such games as shuffleboard, four square, and hopscotch. With a little fencing, part of a parking lot can double as a children's general play area.

The Ultimate Multi-Use Space

A "sanctinasium" is a room that can be used for a wide range of functions from worship services to basketball. Cole Community Church, a large congregation in Boise, Idaho, has chosen to make a sanctinasium the center of its facility complex. Though basically a gymnasium, the facility includes a platform, stage, and baptistry so that it also serves as the worship area and fulfills a variety of other purposes.

The large congregation of Kansas City First Church of the Nazarene built a gymnasium with a movable platform. Both churches use their sanctinasiums for multiple church services, fellowship, recreation, their weekday schools, drama, music, lunch and dinner meetings, activities of teens, seniors, and other groups, plus community meetings. These rooms seldom lie idle. (See appendix A for more on the features of a sanctinasium.)

Except for some offices, almost every room of your church facility can be designed for multiple use, enabling it to be used repeatedly on Sundays and intensively the other six days of the week. Such a design can reduce the amount of floor space needed per person by 40 to 50 percent and reduce the cost of construction proportionally. Because a multi-use building requires so much less of the congregation's time, money, and energy than does a traditional design, it can be one of the most valuable ministry tools your church could have for playing a key role in keeping the church's focus on people rather than buildings.

17

Designing Your Facilities for Outreach

Does the design of your facilities affect how successfully your congregation reaches out to others? While no building can do the work of outreach—buildings do not minister—a building can make a difference. Your building can erect barriers to outreach and service or it can enhance the outreach ministries of your members and help to welcome people.

Take, for example, a building I designed for a church in a small Kansas town. The existing building was on a single residential lot with no parking space and almost no lawn or landscaping. There was nothing impressive about the facility. They really did need to build.

In contrast to the tiny, obscure site of their existing building, the site for the new building provided plenty of space, and the prime location gave me the opportunity to create a significant visual exposure. The focal point of the design was a sanctuary with a high pitched roof. The lawn and trees framed the front of the sanctuary for visual emphasis. The one-story, flat-roofed educational wing was kept low to emphasize the mass and vertical lines of the sanctuary. So that it would not distract from the building's beauty, I hid the parking behind the sanctuary and the educational wing.

Inside the attractive front entryway, a small foyer opened to the parking area on the back, the sanctuary on one side, and the educational wing on the other.

A modest budget required careful design to include all the needed areas. One money saver was that the pastor's study was in the parsonage, so the building needed to include only one small office for records and supplies. The fellowship hall at the far end of the educational wing had a folding wall so it could be divided, and the worship overflow areas had folding walls so they could double as classrooms. At the time I designed this building in the early fifties, folding walls were fairly new, so these were innovative features.

When the building was finished, the members were excited to have a new facility that provided everything they had asked for and more, all for a very reasonable cost. It was work in which I could take justifiable pride.

That building met the needs of its members then and today it still meets their needs. What that building did not do, however, was provide a welcoming environment for newcomers or serve as an effective tool for outreach. It had not occurred to me at the time that it was even possible to design a building for outreach. Because I drew up plans with only the members' needs in mind, I unintentionally built into the design several barriers to outreach, all of them common in traditional church architecture.

Though I had made the front entry the focus of my design, it was not accessible from the parking area. Even behind the building I had provided no visitors' parking. As visitors entered the building, they found themselves in a foyer so small that if someone paused to greet them for more than a few seconds, they would block traffic.

On entering the sanctuary, visitors encountered a half-empty space that gave the impression that not many people cared to attend that church. This resulted from having built the sanctuary big enough to give the congregation room to

179

double and having furnished it with fixed pews. Movable seating would have solved the empty-space problem by making it possible to remove the unneeded chairs.

Worshipers sat in a long, narrow room where they could see only the backs of other people's heads, rather than in a warm, welcoming space where they could see each others' faces and feel a sense of togetherness. Movable seating could have helped with this problem as well.

But the greatest barrier of all was that the church was not open for business except on Sundays and Wednesday evenings. Even when the church was open, this was not obvious to people passing by, because the parking and active entrance were hidden behind the building.

None of these shortcomings interfered with members' needs. The members still found ways to greet one another and make each other feel welcome. The members knew when the church was open for business. The members knew when and where they could reach the pastor any time they needed him. It was only visitors and those who sought the church's ministry during the week, perhaps with crisis needs, who encountered these barriers.

The motivating force of the growing church is serving others, both inside and outside the church body. Our buildings should express that purpose by being user-friendly. This term covers a range of design goals from serving the handicapped to features that invite the "customer" in. Both inside and out, the facilities should say, "We're here to serve you." I helped a congregation in Bakersfield, California, develop a plan for a new church complex that illustrates several ways of doing this.

Invite People In through What They See

The first way a facility can help to welcome people is to invite them in through what they see. The Bakersfield site plan seeks to do this through the following features:

Landscaped visitor parking is in front where it is always visible and available.

The offices are located in front with visitor and other parking areas adjacent to the weekday (office) entry. A canopy marks the entry, puts it in scale with people, and provides shelter, in this case, mostly from the sun. This welcoming design leaves no doubt that this church is open for business all week long.

The church complex is planned so people can see people using the facility all week long. People gather and visit on outdoor terraces placed where passersby can see, not in hidden courtyards.

Glass doors and walls at the large entryways to the fellowship foyer allow people outside to see people inside.

The entrances on both sides of the atrium-like fellowship foyer are serviced by driveways for unloading, with convenient parking nearby. A movable wall between the fellowship foyer and ministry center allows the two spaces to function together when needed.

The design is in scale with people; it uses sizes that make people feel comfortable, not overpowered, dominated, or awed. It avoids strong vertical elements, such as steeples, towers, and campaniles, in favor of horizontal lines and openings. Unlike the Kansas facility that made the sanctuary its visual focus, the large mass formed by the ministry center and fellowship foyer was placed in the center of the site behind the much smaller-scale administration unit.

At another church in the San Francisco area, the site plan includes a soccer field, a picnic grove, and a gym placed at the front of the site where traditionally the sanctuary would be located. A par exercise course is planned for the perimeter of the site for use by the community.

By making the church campus look inviting and open to the community, these congregations hope to announce to their neighbors before they say a word, "We're open for business. You're always welcome here. Membership not required."

Welcome People throughout the Week

When we welcome visitors into our homes, we greet them at the door, on the porch, or in the yard. We invite them in, take their coats and hang them up, and offer them our most comfortable seating. We tell them where their children can be cared for and where the toilet facilities are. We offer them refreshments and do whatever else we can to make them feel at home.

If we truly want people to feel welcome in our churches, we will be no less intentional about welcoming visitors to our church offices during the week. But anyone who tries to exercise this kind of hospitality in a church office is likely to discover quickly that the building was not designed with hospitality in mind. Most churches offer guests little more than a few chairs in the secretarial work space.

To provide a welcoming environment to those who come to the church offices, I recommend a parlor or living room-style reception and waiting room at the entrance to the staff office area. Here visitors can get information, rest, read, or visit, with refreshments available. This room also serves as a control point for entry to the building during the week. The key to making this space work is to staff it with volunteer greeters with big smiles. Outside of office hours this parlor can serve as a bride's room, a funeral family room, or even an evening meeting room if the design carefully considers traffic patterns.

If you are serious about extending a warm welcome to people who visit your office, consider providing a homelike reception parlor.

Welcome People to the Services

Your building should have one or more welcoming entrances for visitors to your services, entrances with a human scale that are convenient to visitor parking. I recommend a greeting alcove just inside the entrances, an area where greeters can invite visitors to step out of the flow of traffic, be comfortably seated, and be welcomed in a friendship zone designed for that purpose.

This alcove should be part of the large fellowship foyer described in chapter 16 through which people enter the worship area. This fellowship foyer is a key element in creating a welcoming environment, designed to promote fellowship among members and visitors before and after worship and other gatherings.

Traditionally the church has consigned "fellowship" to a room called a fellowship hall in the remotest part of the building. Fellowship, though, is not peripheral to the life of the church but essential. Without fellowship we have no church. To centrally locate a large fellowship foyer helps to integrate fellowship into the total life of the church rather than treat it as a separate, and perhaps optional, function of the body.

Of course many churches with buildings that have traditional designs have been effective in reaching out to welcome new people into the fellowship, because the people have committed themselves to serving others. But if yours is that kind of a church, a church with a heart to serve, which kind of building would you rather have—one that erects obstacles to hospitality or one that invites people in through what they see and offers a welcoming environment to all who come, whether during office hours or to services?

You can have a building that helps you say, "We're here to serve. Come on in."

Conclusion

Releasing the Church to Change the World

Sometimes I ask a congregation, "How much do you expect to spend on your next building program? What might happen if, instead of spending it on a new building, you raised that same amount in cash and pledges to minister to the needs of people right here in your own community?"

Imagine with me. Imagine that the year is 2040 and that over the intervening years thousands of churches have dared to accept this challenge. They have adopted the *principle of use:* They will not build any new facilities until they are using their existing facilities as fully as possible. It has become commonplace for churches to have not just double worship services but three, four, even five services. Virtually every square foot of space in every church building has been designed or remodeled so it can be used for a variety of purposes all week long. As a result, churches grow to two, three, even four times the size they once did before they need additional buildings.

Imagine that these same churches have long since converted from debt financing to provision financing. Because they no longer have interest expense, the amount they spend on construction is only about a third of what it would have been if they had borrowed the money.

Now imagine that these churches have taken all the money saved by not building unnecessary buildings and by not paying interest and have invested that amount in ministering to the needs of people in their own neighborhoods or nearby communities. What would these churches be like now?

Imagine a church in a small farm community where restless youth look for something to do on Saturday night, where people often grow lonely as they grow older, where limited economic opportunities leave hardworking families helpless during economic downturns, where the everybody-knows-everybody-else's-business atmosphere compounds the pain of being fired, of chemical dependency, of divorce. Once such a church has redirected its focus from building to meeting the needs of people, how will the church have changed? How will the changed church have changed the community?

Think of a church in an affluent suburban neighborhood. After they drew the line on building, they redirected their time, energy, and money into reaching out to the needs of those who lived there. All kinds of support groups sprang up: AA, AlAnon, Divorce Recovery, Cancer Recovery. Members developed ministries to help restore hurting marriages and help parents reestablish relationships with alienated children. The church began to provide finances and volunteers for a variety of ministries in a nearby low-income neighborhood. Throughout the community the church became known as a group of people who have their fingers firmly on the pulse of the community's needs and who reach out creatively and compassionately to meet those needs.

Or imagine an inner-city congregation whose limited resources are straining to respond to poverty, single-parent homes, child abuse, chemical dependency, unsafe housing, and despair. Most such churches already have a long record of creative and intensive use of facilities. But what would happen in this congregation if churches from surrounding suburbs redirected hundreds of thousands of dollars that traditionally would have been spent on church buildings to help them minister to these desperate needs?

Imagining three such churches is easy. After all, churches like these are around, and we all admire them. But now imagine that by the year 2040 half the churches in your city or town look like this. No, they are not all cut out of the same mold. Each congregation has unique ministries that grow out of the needs of its neighbors and the gifts and callings of its members. Yet they all share this in common: They no longer consider bigger or more impressive buildings to be signs of success. All that matters is to minister to people's needs by the power of Christ.

If that were true of just half the churches of your community, how would your community be changed? Can you imagine it? What new or expanded services would be available to the elderly? To the unemployed? To abused children and those who abuse them? How would life be different for single teenage moms in your community? How many more promising young people from underprivileged homes would receive technical training or go to college?

What new opportunities would be available to those who seek drug rehabilitation? For students who need extra tutoring? For the medically underserved? For those living in substandard housing? For those needing job training or financial counseling?

If all these tangible expressions of caring had sprung up in your community, some from your church, most from others, what differences might you see in the juvenile delinquency rate? In the crime rate? In the unemployment rate? In the divorce rate?

What would it have meant for the people in your congregation to be personally involved, week after week, in compassionate ministries to hurting people? To have seen God work through them to bring comfort and healing? To have encountered God in those they served, and to have been surprised again and again by being ministered to in the act of ministering? To have worked hand in hand in ministries to the community with Christians of many denominations—Baptists and Roman Catholics, Nazarenes and United Methodists, Assemblies of God and Presbyterians—all united by love of God and love of neighbor?

If half the churches in your community made the commitment to redirect three-fourths of their construction funds to meet the needs of people right in your own community, and all these ministries grew out of that commitment, how would that change how your community sees the church? How much more open to the gospel might the unchurched be? What effect might that have on the size of the churches in your town?

Now, multiply that image by thousands. What if the transformation you have just envisioned for your own community were duplicated in every community in your state or province? What if half of all the churches in every town in the United States and Canada caught this vision and determined never again to let buildings become their focus, not even temporarily? How would our society be changed?

It's difficult to imagine anything approaching this without envisioning one of the greatest revivals of all time. By the millions our neighbors would be struck with the truth that Christianity is not some special interest group seeking to promote its own success but a radically caring community of people who have tapped into a power that can meet their deepest needs and change their lives.

No more powerful force in the war on drugs would exist than the power of the church. There would be no more powerful force in the battle against unemployment than the church. Politicians in Ottawa and Washington would talk about what to do with the "church dividend," the hundreds of billions of dollars no longer needed for government social programs because the church once again was taking its rightful place in meeting the needs of people, and doing so far more effectively than the government ever had been able to do. This would echo the days of the early Christian church.

Had the churches of the first and second centuries focused on buildings, such a witness as theirs never would have taken place. But because they focused on meeting the needs of people by God's power, the world sat up and took notice.

There is no reason that the church today cannot recover the vitality of that early church. Our nations can be changed by God's love. Your city or town can be transformed. But it will never happen on the scale it needs to happen until we change the way we think about church buildings, until we realize that building buildings is not the work of the church, that at best buildings are only tools that can help us with the work of the church to meet people's needs through the power and love of Christ.

Appendix A

How to Write a Program of Needs for Your Church Facilities

Your architect cannot design in a vacuum. Without knowing the specific needs of your church, some architects will rely on traditional designs developed for the maintenance (nongrowing) church, designs that do not take into account the special design requirements of a fast-growing congregation. Traditionally architects are not trained to design for the growing church, so it is up to the church-growth committee, or whatever you call the group responsible to plan your facility needs, to give your architect clear direction. (For help on how to form this committee, review chapter 15.)

The tool you create to direct your architect is called a *program of needs*. This is a written document based on realistic projections of growth. It itemizes facility needs and desires for all the functions of your church: worship and other large group gatherings, fellowship, education, administration, recreation, and parking. It describes how different parts of the building are to relate to each other, to entrances, to parking, and to streets. It includes any equipment, furnishings, or other special requirements that the committee wants incorporated into the design. It specifies design needs that grow out of the liturgy of your faith tradition or denomination.

As a part of writing your program, visit at least one or two fast-growing churches, preferably of your own denomination, that have been built recently. Find out which aspects of their facilities work well and which do not, and incorporate what you learn into your plan.

Keep in mind that the growth committee does not design a building; it only defines what it wants the building to do. It is the architect's job to design a building to meet all these needs. Even so, preparation of a program of needs is a demanding task and in some cases will require the help of a professional—a church facility consultant or architect who understands the special needs of growing churches.

Which of the concepts described both below and in the referenced portions of the book are practical and desirable for your congregation? Go through the book and highlight each of the features you want to incorporate into your design.

Which concepts are not practical or desirable for your situation? Go through the book and mark each of these items with an X. Then, as a committee, develop and write out an alternate plan for these aspects of your program of need.

Finally, give your architect your highlighted copy of this book along with the supplemental plans you have written. Together, these make up your program of need. Of course, if you prefer, you can combine the highlighted features from the book and your supplemental plans into a single document for the architect. If you use any of the special features advocated in this book, however, it is essential that you have your architect read the book so he or she will clearly understand the purpose of those features and how they are to relate to the rest of the building.

The following outline can guide you in drawing up your church's program of needs. It incorporates features specifically designed to meet the needs of the growing church—high-intensity multiple use of space and features intended to facilitate outreach. If you plan for an entirely new facility, you can incorporate as many of these features as you wish. If you remodel or build an addition, you will still be able to adopt many of these concepts, though with some limitations. Even if you meet in a rented facility, you should be able to come up with significant ways to improve on your use and configuration of space to allow for growth.

After becoming familiar with the following outline, the church-growth committee should consider individually each of the seven areas described.

Ministry Center

We recommend that the growing church build not a traditional sanctuary but a ministry center. Refer to chapter 16 for a description of how this multi-use space can work.

If you choose to create a ministry center, you have two major decisions to make. First, how many services do you plan to hold? Your answer to this question will largely determine the size of this space. Second, what functions will take place in this space? Your answer to this question will determine your needs for equipment, movable versus fixed staging, lighting, acoustical treatment and sound system, and active storage adjacent to the room.

Key to making the ministry center concept work is the use of movable church chairs for seating. Church chairs are stored by stacking, not folding. They are upholstered, more comfortable than pews, have wood or steel frames, and are designed to gang together. They will probably cost more than pews but are worth it, because they increase your seating capacity as well as make the room usable for multiple ministries throughout the week. They are available with book racks, communion cup holders, and envelope racks.

If your church wishes to consider the sanctinasium option for a ministry center (see end of chapter 16), you should be aware of the following requirements for making such a facility workable:

- A gym-type carpeted floor
- Acoustical treatment for speaking and music
- A sound system designed for this space, with a movable console
- A dual lighting system: high-intensity lighting for recreation; for worship and other uses, appropriate lighting that can be dimmed, together with theatrical lighting and controls for the platform area
- Large active storage rooms for equipment and furniture
- Preparation rooms for drama and other programs
- Dressing rooms for recreation

The key to making a sanctinasium work is to design it primarily to satisfy the needs of worship and other services, including the gym functions, rather than to design a typical gym and then use it for worship.

Fellowship Foyer

For the growing church we recommend a fellowship foyer that combines the functions of the traditional foyer and the traditional fellowship hall. It is often practical to build a fellowship foyer as an addition to an existing building. When a church wishes to go to multiple services in a building designed for single services, the addition of a fellowship foyer may be essential to make multiple services practical. For the multi-use and traffic-flow functions of the fellowship foyer, see chapter 16. For the welcoming and outreach functions of the fellowship foyer, see chapter 17.

If you choose to include a fellowship foyer in your design, a major decision you face is whether to include a movable wall system so that in addition to its use as a foyer and fellowship hall, some or all of the space can be used for small groups and classes.

Educational Functions

The kind of space needed for educational use varies with the age group. Modify the following recommendations to meet the needs of your church.

Nursery

If the church serves young families, careful planning of the nursery area should be a high priority. For many parents with nursery-age children, an excellent nursery and staff is the single most important factor in choosing a church home.

The nursery should be easily accessible from the visitors' parking lot and not too close to the ministry center. Provide extra corridor space at the entrances to the nursery rooms so parents can pick up their children without entering the rooms.

Design separate spaces for toddlers, crawlers, and crib babies, with each room having a maximum capacity of twelve to fifteen children plus workers. If possible, provide a sleeping room just off the crib room that is completely visible to crib room workers. A room where mothers can care for and feed their children should have its own entrance so mothers need not go through the nursery.

Equip each room with individual cubicles for each child's personal items, including diaper bags, just inside the door. Each room should have an adult-size toilet, counter, and sink. Have a storage closet for toys, supplies, folding play pens, and other equipment in each room.

Children

While rows of small rooms work well for children's classes in small churches, in the larger church large flexible spaces are more practical.

Movable sight breaks and storage units on wheels can be arranged to subdivide open spaces for age groupings. A single-age group can grow to thirty or forty in one room if the adult-to-student ratio is appropriate for the age.

The master-teacher/worker approach is a practical way to staff such classes. Each room is supervised by a master teacher who is assisted by one worker for each four to five preschoolers, each five to six primaries, or each eight to ten older children. Workers serve as caregivers at tables or in activity groups and help to maintain control when the whole group is assembled.

Design of this kind of classroom should include excellent sound absorption, a work counter with a sink and drinking fountain, and a toilet facility so children need not leave the room or area.

Teens

There appears to be no upper limit to the size of the junior high or senior high departments. The bigger the group, the better the teens seem to like it. Large churches that have tried to divide the teens (into two sessions of Sunday school, for example) have usually found it does not work; the teens all gravitate to one session. The best way to accommodate a growing teen ministry, therefore, seems to be to provide larger rooms as the teen group grows. This makes planning facilities for a growing youth group a challenge.

One solution is to use a movable sound-wall system. Another is to plan walls that can be removed for growth into adjacent space. (You can build and remove inexpensive gypsum walls several times before their cost will equal the cost of a sound-wall system.) Or you can plan a variety of room sizes and move the group to ever-larger rooms as needed. Whichever solution you choose, it is critical to design the room for high decibel levels (what adults call noise).

Like other parts of the building, the teen meeting areas should be designed for intensive use during the week. This requires large storage rooms for the various furnishings and equipment used in youth ministry. An outside entrance to the area, a serving kitchen, and toilet facilities are all important to weekday utilization.

Successful use of a gymnasium as the primary meeting space for teens is difficult to achieve. It may be possible by using gym-type carpet, acoustical treatment, a movable sound system, a dual lighting system, plus enough storage to make a gym work. Most churches will have more practical, cost-effective alternatives.

Adults

Facility requirements for adult classes vary from church to church. One congregation had only two adult classes of several hundred each, both taught lecture style by master teachers. Another church tried to keep classes in a range of thirty to sixty so each would function as a "congregation" within the larger church. The more common pattern is to have a variety of class sizes and different styles of teaching. If you have any special classes that require something other than the usual rectangular room, the needs of those classes must figure into your design. The building plan should follow the teaching plan to be used, not vice versa.

Space Allowances

The following space allowances are in common use and can guide you in determining your space needs for education. Teachers and workers are counted along with their students. Space allowances are based on average attendance and allow room for 20 percent growth and occasional higher attendance. Area is based on wall-to-wall measurements.

Age Group	Range of Needed Space
Nursery, preschool, and kindergarten	30 sq. ft. per person 35 sq. ft. with large equipment 25 sq. ft. minimum
Children	
Lower grades	25 sq. ft. each 20 sq. ft. minimum
Upper grades	20 sq. ft. each 15 sq. ft. minimum
Teens	
Class only	15 sq. ft. each (with tables)
Total multi-use	20 sq. ft. each
Adults	
At tables	15 sq. ft. each
Lecture class	12 sq. ft. each 10 sq. ft. minimum

The total building area needed for classrooms, walls, corridors, toilets, mechanical, janitor, and storage is close to 50 square feet per person, based on average attendance and single use of the facility.

Study the space utilization of your present classes based on average attendance and adjust the above allowances to your specific methods and needs. The space needed per person is determined primarily by the method of teaching, type of furniture, and how the furniture is arranged. Identify space wasters—large tables with seating on just one side, a large room with seating only around the walls, or big overstuffed divans and chairs.

A note on tables: Buy the best, strongest folding tables available; it saves money in the long run. Buy six-foot tables (maximum size) so one person can fold and stack them. They are the best size for children's classes, seating six per table plus the teacher and a guest if needed. This size also gangs together best.

Make sure all tables are adjustable in height so they can be changed quickly from children's use to adults' and back again.

Administration

The most important requirement for administrative space is to gather all professional ministry staff and support staff offices into a single administrative suite. This is important for efficiency, teamwork, and accountability, as well as to enable all staff members to be easily available to the public—a key component of being open for business. The offices should be close to work areas, a copy machine, a conference room, and other facilities used in common.

The offices should be in the front part of the building, highly visible, with convenient parking, easy to enter, and totally user-friendly. The entryway should be designed to say "welcome." If possible, the church that is determined to offer a welcoming environment to those it serves should provide a comfortable, parlorlike hospitality area for office visitors just inside the weekday (office) entrance. Chapter 17 describes this feature in more detail.

For planning purposes, use a ratio of one professional ministry staff member per 150 in average worship attendance unless you have developed your own ratio. Keep in mind that staff is added ahead of the next growth phase. A ratio of one support staff member for every two professional staff members is minimum if the professionals are to spend their time doing what they are educated and trained for rather than doing work that secretaries can do faster and better. The facility plan must provide for future expansion of the administrative area as growth requires, either by changing the function of adjacent space to administration or by constructing an addition to the building.

One facility need almost always overlooked is space for lay ministry staff. Every growing congregation has members willing to serve in support roles. They need places to work with the assistance and supervision of the professional and support staff. This work space may include telephones for outreach and follow-up, an area for lay counseling, or work space to prepare mailings. The church that takes the ministry of the laity seriously enough to provide office space and equipment for its lay ministers is more likely to be a growing church.

For more specific suggestions on how to make your administrative space "open for business," review chapter 8. Also see chapter 11 for ideas on minimizing administrative space and enhancing staff performance with the semi-virtual office.

Recreation

In the forties and fifties many churches said, "We want to minister to the youth of our church and community, so design us a *youth center.*" In the sixties and seventies the big thrust was to build a *recreation center.* In the eighties and nineties the *family life center* was where the action was. I wonder what name we will invent next to describe what we build, because for all of the above we have built *gymnasiums.*

The motives behind this were all great, but most of these churches built buildings to house nonexistent ministries. They assumed that if they built the buildings, people would use them. But most of the time the buildings lay unused.

Consider building a gymnasium only if the church already has a strong, successful ministry that uses recreation and if other facilities are not available. Do a careful cost-effectiveness study before deciding on a gymnasium. To be cost-effective, it must be a multi-use facility, and that requires a first-class, expensive building. (See the discussion of educational space for teens earlier in this appendix for the basic features needed in a multipurpose gymnasium.) A bare-bones gym is a poor investment, because it will have very limited use.

We have yet to witness a church using a recreational program as an effective ministry for outreach. We have seen some limited success with softball and basketball. The potential is there for a ministry, but remember: Create the ministry first, then build the facility.

In considering recreational needs, keep in mind that paved parking can, for minimal cost, be designed for basketball, volleyball, tennis, and other recreational uses.

Parking

Growth is stopped by the shortage of parking more often than by any other single facility requirement. A ratio of one car for every 2.5 people works in most areas. To find out what the car-to-people ratio is in your church, count all the people in the building (including children, of course) and all the cars parked at the church. In your planning, assume that the ratio will go down and require proportionally more parking spaces in the future. A ratio of one car for every 2 people, or even less, applies in some areas.

Without landscaping, you can park about 120 cars per acre; about 100 per acre with landscaping. With compact spaces the ratio may be increased. Most cities and counties have specific parking space requirements, such as landscaping and control of water runoff.

When you consider parking options, particularly at existing sites, don't forget to consider alternative approaches: remote parking with shuttle service, stacked parking, getting multiple use out of parking space by having multiple services. Remember that worship and education classes cannot be held at the same time unless there is enough parking for both. (See chapter 6 to review parking options.)

External Appearance

The outward appearance of your facilities, including the scale of the building, location of offices, location of parking, location of recreational facilities, entryways, and landscaping, makes a statement to the community. It can say, "We're number one," an intimidating message; or it can say, "We're open for business, and you're always welcome."

Study chapter 17 as you consider how to design the appearance of your building, parking, and grounds to express the message you truly want to communicate.

Once your growth committee has written up your program of needs in the above seven areas (plus other areas required by your church's particular needs, such as music rehearsal), you are ready to show your program to your architect. Some churches will need to hire a consultant to help them develop a facility plan to the point that it is ready to be taken to an architect. Since your architect may not have been trained in many of the concepts described in this book—particularly high-intensity, multi-use design and a building designed primarily for others rather than for the members—you will need to employ an architect who is flexible and who enjoys developing innovative solutions to architectural challenges.

By basing his or her work on the detailed program of needs your committee has created guided by this outline, your architect should be able to design facilities almost ideally suited to your congregation's needs and goals.

Appendix B

Director of Ministry Development

More and more, churches want to hire staff to be equippers of ministers rather than "ministers for hire." Ideally every member of the pastoral and program staff should approach his or her work as an equipper. Realistically, though, a pastoral staff member who has functioned primarily as a caregiver may not be able to change ministry styles overnight and may not have the gifts needed to design and implement a strong equipping system.

Sometimes a useful step in developing a stronger equipping system is to hire a staff member—or empower a volunteer—to design and direct such a system. Such a position is increasingly common on church staffs. Some churches call this person the director of lay ministries; others, the minister of ministries. We are calling it director of ministry development.

What does a director of ministry development do? What kind of person should you look for in hiring a director of ministry development? Either of the following job descriptions—one for a full-time position, the other for a part-time or volunteer position—can serve as a starting point, but it must be tailored to the gifts and call of the staff person as well as to the needs of the church.

The full-time position includes two primary areas of responsibility— working with ministry teams and working with small groups. In some cases it will work better for one person (staff or volunteer) to work with ministry team development and support and for another person to coordinate small groups. Sometimes one or the other of these responsibilities can be incorporated into the job description of a present staff member.

Few churches will implement both ministry teams and a small-group ministry simultaneously, so in some cases it may work best to start with a half-time position focusing on one kind of group, then expanding the job to add the other area later on.

An organization that provides training and resources for directors of ministry development (they call them directors of lay ministries) is Leadership Network. Contact them at 2501 Cedar Springs LB-5, Suite 200, Dallas, TX 75201; 800-765-5323; www.leadnet.org/

Job Description: Full-Time Position

Focus

1. Implement equipping ministries to make all the youth and adults in the congregation aware that God has called them to be ministers, to deepen their understanding of the nature of ministry beyond traditional roles in the church, to guide them in identifying their personal calls and identifying spiritual gifts, to facilitate the formation of ministry teams, to provide a support system for the nurture of ministry teams, and to provide through the local church or outside resources training for a wide variety of ministries so every member can be well equipped for ministry.

2. Implement and oversee a system of recruiting, training, and continuing coaching for small-group leaders. Seek to increase participation in small groups and the quality of small-group leadership until 80 to 95 percent of all pastoral care in the congregation is being handled by small-group leaders and intern leaders.

Responsibilities

1. Develop and implement a comprehensive strategy for equipping members for ministry (see Focus statement 1 under Focus). This will include the development of a "core curriculum," which all adult members will be urged to complete and which all new members will complete as part of coming into membership. The core curriculum should include practical teaching on lay ministry (such as *The Lay Ministry Revolution* by Eddy Hall and Gary Morsch, Baker, 1995) and on identifying spiritual gifts and call.

Eventually this should also include a clearly defined process through which self-organizing ministry teams can be birthed and nurtured along with the staff support for these ministry teams.

2. Develop and implement a system for individualized call and gift discernment and assistance as needed in ministry placement. Whether through small groups or through a team of trained volunteer counselors, each member of the congregation will be invited to work at a guided process of identifying personal call and spiritual gifts. These people will then be offered assistance as needed in matching their gifts and call to existing ministry opportunities within or outside of the church, or, if a good match doesn't exist, will be coached and assisted in the process of creating a ministry that will allow them to fulfill call. The goal of this process is not to "fill the slots" in the church's existing structures but to enable people to do ministry that grows out of their own personal sense of call.

3. Develop and implement a comprehensive strategy for small-group care. This person will develop a system for training/coaching small-group leaders, for recruiting intern leaders, and for multiplication of groups. Training of small-group leaders should involve a combination of on-the-job training as intern leaders, regular meetings with a coach, formal training in the local church, and possibly small-group leadership training at workshops outside the local church. The staff member will personally equip and coordinate the coaches of small-group leaders who will in turn equip and supervise the small-group leaders. This person should also lead the church in making small groups entry points for people coming into the church by teaching/showing small groups how to do small-group–based friendship evangelism.

Note: This person should not be hired to take over the work of your Sunday school superintendent, your Christian education council, or any other group that is administering existing programs, nor is this person responsible to recruit people to fill positions.

Qualifications

1. Passionate vision for every-member ministry. This person must believe passionately that every member of the church is called to ministry and have a compelling desire to mobilize all the people of the church for ministry, helping each find his or her place of call in ministry, either within the church or in the community.

2. Experience in holistic small groups. Since this person is responsible to guide and oversee the church's small-group ministries, he or she needs to have significant experience and expertise in this area. If the person has a strong commitment to small groups but no formal training in how to develop a churchwide small-groups ministry, the church can pay for this person to receive appropriate training shortly after assuming the position.

3. A demonstrated commitment to friendship evangelism. This should be a person who consistently and intentionally nurtures friendships with non-Christians for the purpose of ministry to them, and who does this in a winsome, nonoffensive way.

4. Empowering leadership. This must be the kind of person who inspires others to be all they can be and who encourages them to take risks without being paralyzed by fear of failure. This person should have a record of enabling others to fulfill their potential.

5. A layperson's perspective. In most cases the best candidate for this job is a layperson, not a career pastor. This person most often comes from within the congregation.

6. An entrepreneurial management style. This person may be an entrepreneur and must at least think like an entrepreneur. This person's management style must reflect creativity, not a preference for maintaining the status quo. This person must thrive on innovation and starting new ventures and he or she will probably be bored with maintaining a project once it is up and running. He or she must have demonstrated expertise in coaching others through the start-up phase of new ventures.

7. Teaching ability. Since equipping is at the heart of this role, this person must be a strong mentor whose teaching style emphasizes clear practical application, not abstract theory. While this person may be asked to teach occasionally during a worship service, especially when the church is focusing on lay ministry, preaching normally would not be a high priority for this staff position.

8. Ability to resource other staff members. This person is not the only member of the staff responsible to equip members for ministry. In a church with other associate pastoral staff, this person can be an "equipper of equippers," equipping other staff members to become more effective in their equipping ministries. For example, this person could work with an associate pastor for children to help her or him equip all those in the church who work in ministry to children. This can include assistance in testing for spiritual gifts, in matching people to the positions that fit their calls and their gifts, in advising on possible restructuring of ministry programs so the programs make better use of the available gift mix, or streamlining programs when the number of "slots" exceeds the number of people who are gifted and called to a given ministry. This person can also work with associate staff in helping them guide the birth and operation of self-organizing ministry teams in their areas of responsibility.

Job Description: Volunteer or Part-Time Position

Focus

Implement equipping ministries to make all the youth and adults in the congregation aware that God has called them to be ministers, to deepen their understanding of the nature of ministry beyond traditional roles in the church, to guide them in identifying their personal calls and identifying spiritual gifts, to facilitate the formation of ministry teams, to provide a support system for the nurture of ministry teams, and to provide through the local church or outside resources training for a wide variety of ministries so every member can be well equipped for ministry. This part-time position requires 10–25 hours per week.

Responsibilities

1. Develop and implement a comprehensive strategy for equipping members for ministry. This will include the development of a curriculum that includes practical teaching on lay ministry (such as *The Lay Ministry Revolution*) and on identifying spiritual gifts and call.

Eventually this should also include a clearly defined process by which self-organizing ministry teams can be birthed and nurtured along with the staff support for these ministry teams.

2. Develop and implement a system for individualized call and gift discernment and assistance as needed in ministry placement. Whether through small groups or through a team of trained volunteer counselors, each member of the congregation will be invited to work at a guided process of identifying personal call and spiritual gifts. These people will then be offered assistance as needed in matching their gifts and call to existing ministry opportunities within or outside of the church, or, if a good match doesn't exist, will be coached and assisted in the process of creating a ministry that will allow them to fulfill call. The goal of this process is not to "fill the slots" in the church's existing structures but to enable people to do ministry that grows out of their own personal sense of call.

Qualifications

1. Passionate vision for every-member ministry. This person must believe passionately that every member of the church is called to ministry and have a compelling desire to mobilize all the people of the church for ministry, helping each find his or her place of call in ministry, either within the church or in the community.

2. Empowering leadership. This must be the kind of person who inspires others to be all they can be and who encourages them to take risks without being paralyzed by fear of failure. This person should have a record of enabling others to fulfill their potential.

3. A layperson's perspective. In most cases the best candidate for this job is a layperson, not a career pastor. This person most often comes from within the congregation.

4. An entrepreneurial management style. This person may be an entrepreneur and must at least think like an entrepreneur. This person's management style must reflect creativity, not a preference for maintaining the status quo. This person must thrive on innovation and starting new ventures and he or she will probably be bored with maintaining a project once it is up and running. He or she must have demonstrated expertise in coaching others through the start-up phase of new ventures.

5. Teaching ability. Since equipping is at the heart of this role, this person must be a strong mentor whose teaching style emphasizes clear practical application, not abstract theory. While this person may be asked to teach occasionally during a worship service, especially when the church is focusing on lay ministry, preaching normally would not be a high priority for this staff position.

Notes

Chapter 1 *Confessions of a Surprised Architect*

1. Richard Foster, *The Freedom of Simplicity* (San Francisco: Harper & Row, 1981), 153–54.

Chapter 2 *Can Buildings Kill Church Growth?*

1. Throughout this book, names of congregations have been changed except when the town where the church is located is named.

Chapter 10 *The Overprogramming Trap*

1. A tool designed to help members of congregations gain a broader perspective on ministry, discern personal call, and form call-based ministry teams is *The Lay Ministry Revolution: How You Can Join* by Eddy Hall and Gary Morsch (Grand Rapids: Baker, 1995).

2. Sue Mallory, "Lay Ministries outside the Church," *Into Action* (October 1997), 7.

3. Elizabeth O'Connor, *Cry Pain, Cry Hope* (Waco, Tex.: Word, 1987), 81–82.

Chapter 11 *Beyond Facility-Based Ministry*

1. Rick Warren, *The Purpose Driven Church* (Grand Rapids: Zondervan, 1995), 46.

2. One provider of such services is Portable Church Industries, 1260 Kempar St., Madison Heights, MI 48071. Phone: 800-939-7722. Web: www. portablechurch.com.

3. Lawrence Richards, *Children's Ministry: Nurturing Faith within the Family of God* (Grand Rapids: Zondervan, 1983).

4. Training resources—books, audiotapes, and videotapes—for intergenerational small-group leaders, as well as intergenerational curricular resources, are available through Touch Publications, P. O. Box 19888, Houston, TX 77224. Phone: 800-735-5865. Web: www.touchusa.org. Another good source for intergenerational cell curriculum is Allen Thomas Publishing, P. O. Box 40269, Nashville, TN 37204. Phone: 615-385-9073.

5. Colonial Hills Baptist Church, "A Review of Our Pastor's Vision," *The Link* 1, no. 1.

Chapter 12 *Good Intentions Are Not Enough*

1. Larry Burkett, *Should Churches Borrow Money?* (Tucker, Ga.: Christian Financial Concepts, 1978), pamphlet.

2. Virgil Vogt, *Treasure in Heaven* (Ann Arbor, Mich.: Servant Books, 1982), 92–93.

Chapter 14 *Turning Church Spending Right Side Up*

1. Eberhard Arnold, *The Early Christians,* trans. and ed. Society of Brothers (1970; reprint, Grand Rapids: Baker, 1979), 18–19.

Acknowledgments

I (Ray) wish to thank first of all my wife, Sally, who has been a colaborer with me in our consulting ministry since it began in 1980. In our work with churches, her gifts have consistently compensated for certain of my weaknesses. As a partner on the consulting team, she has played a critical role in developing many of the concepts that appear in these pages and has, of course, been deeply involved in shaping the manuscript.

I want to thank James N. Posey who introduced me to the principles of biblical finance, on which part 3 of this book is based, and who provided encouragement—and on two occasions office space—for the writing process. I thank Shirley Posey who volunteered her able services as proofreader and copy editor of the manuscript. Elizabeth Ketner, my mother-in-law, allowed us to set up office in her home and extended warm hospitality during the writing of part of the book, which I enjoyed and appreciated.

Many people contributed to this book by influencing my thinking with their books, tapes, or personal contact. Principal among these are Howard Chambers through his pastoral work; Ray Stedman through his writings, tapes, and speaking; Win Arn and Charles Arn through their writing and seminars; Peter Wagner and Carl George through their writing and teaching; and Joseph Aldridge, Richard Foster, and Larry Burkett through their writing.

We both thank Paul Engle, our editor, for his belief in the importance of the message of this book and his encouragement and practical assistance to us through the years.

Most of all, we thank God who called us into this challenging ministry and who has given us the opportunity to learn from the churches we have worked with many exciting concepts and practical ideas we could have learned no other way.

═══════════════   ═══════════════

Ray Bowman and Eddy Hall lead Living Stones Associates, a team of church consultants that works with churches to enhance ministry through integrated planning of ministries, staffing, facilities, and finances; through equipping events for church leadership teams and congregations; and through coaching pastors and church staff.

During thirty years as an architect, Bowman designed many churches and other buildings before leaving his architectural firm to become a consultant. Hall, a freelance writer and editor for almost thirty years, has been collaborating with Bowman since 1986 on articles and books growing out of his consulting work. In 1996 he joined Bowman as an associate consultant.

The authors have also written *When Not to Borrow: Unconventional Financial Wisdom to Set Your Church Free*. Their articles have appeared in more than 40 periodicals.

For more information on church consulting services, contact:

Ray Bowman Consulting/Living Stones Associates
4526 Sentinel Rock Terrace
Larkspur, CO 80118
Phone: 303-681-3543

Eddy Hall Consulting/Living Stones Associates
101 South Pine Road
Goessel, KS 67053
Phone: 316-367-2689
E-mail: eddyhall@futureks.net

Or visit the Living Stones Associates Web site:
www.living-stones.com